# REVERSING REJECTION

## — & LOW —

# SELF-ESTEEM

---❖---

## FREEDOM
### FROM THE CLUTCHES
### OF THE ENEMY

# JOEL BISHOP

*This book is in dedication to everyone desperate for a new season of compelling motivation in their mindset. It is also committed to everyone looking for positive character reinforcement to continue to promote constructive feelings toward oneself and others.*

# TABLE OF CONTENTS

# ACKNOWLEDGMENTS

In humble adoration, I want to first give thanks to my inspiration, Jesus Christ, the Saviour, Protector and Sustainer of my life. He has commissioned me by His Spirit to motivate and bless those experiencing rejection and low self-esteem with the knowledge of this book

With sincere appreciation, I would like to thank my beloved sister in the faith, Norma Reid for taking time out from her busy schedule to contribute to the editing of this craft.

I also want to thank the beautiful wife of my youth, Alicia, who has been a great motivation for my aspiration. I have been blessed tremendously to have her as the mother of our four children.

I want to extend thanks to all six of my children, Joel, Elijah, Jolissa, Nathaniel, Johannah and Godswill for their favourable words of encouragement and support.

I also want to thank my church family at Kingdom House of Worship. I have been lifted in prayers and embraced in friendship concerning this endeavour. It is with a grateful heart I am saying thanks in advance to everyone who will purchase this book, and help to excel it to great success. I pray that God will bless you for your support as your lives become enriched with each reading.

# INTRODUCTION

Rejection and low Self-esteem have infected all of humanity through Adam and Eve's disobedience and betrayal of faith in the Most High God. In spite of their disastrous conduct, we are not subjects of rejection and its symptoms. Jesus Christ came in the flesh and allowed himself to become crucified on the cross. So that through his shed blood and resurrection, all of humankind would have the privilege to become free from the powers of rejection and low self-esteem. If you do not know your God-given rights and liberties, then you will subject your mind, body and spirit to accept inferior and illegal treatment throughout your life-span. It's your right to be joyful and live in freedom from rejection, low self-esteem and all of their destructive effects.

It is decisive on our part as believers to understand that to de-throne rejection and low self-esteem from our mindset; it requires mandatory belief in the Holy Scriptures. Be cautious not to trust in the proclamation of rejection and low self-esteem. Adam made a conscious decision to disobey God's directives and commands for his life. By so doing, he allowed rejection to reign supreme over the human race. To live a victorious life in Christ Jesus, free from Rejection and its influences, we must acquire a renewed mind-set. A complete turnaround from the ineffective feelings to which we have become accustomed is required. ***Romans 12:2 says*** this **"And be not conformed to this world: but be ye transformed by the renewing of your mind, that ye may prove what is good, and acceptable, and perfect, will of God."**

If you fail to transform your mindset from negative to posi-tive, then you will not be able to distinguish between which thoughts and imaginations you should approve or decline.

Decide to be of a joyful heart in every hardship always.

If God disapproves of something, do not allow it to enter into your mind. All ideas or intentions must become tested before they are made manifest. As human beings, we can become prone to all forms of emotions. However, we must be diligent and practice caution, so as not to engage with negative emotions that subject us to rejection and low self- esteem. We must seek to know the will of God and embrace positive feelings consistently.

This book is designed to impart the knowledge and understanding of the harsh and destructive reality that Rejection and Low Self-esteem can have on the human mind, body and soul. Once you take the time to read this book, comprehend the contents, and be willing to apply the directed suggestions and strategies, you will rise above your current harmful emotional barriers. It will also set you on a pathway of wisdom, faith, courage and strength, which will assist you in attaining the spiritual level that God intended for you.

When it looks like and feels as if nothing is happening in your life, practice to be of good courage and don't abandon, your heart's desire, faith and hope in God. *Psalm 37:4 (KJV)* **says to delight thyself also in the LORD, and he shall give you the desire of your heart.** It is not the will of God for you to live in bondage to any form of rejection or low self-esteem. Be confident that you are God's inheritance. *Psalm 94:14 (NIV) declares, "For the* **Lord will not reject his people; He will never forsake his inheritance."** He allowed his blood to shed for you to ensure that you will have life abundantly in Him. It was also for you to glory in his everlasting peace, love, joy and happiness.

*Don't stop reading;*
*there is a blessing in this book for You!*

# THE ORIGIN OF REJECTION

The first manifestation of Rejection and its assignment began in Heaven, and was showcase through Lucifer's pride, as a weapon of termination, against the Lord God, who created him. The second manifestation of rejection occurred on earth in the Garden of Eden. Lucifer was formed perfectly as a beautifully anointed cherub, but at some point in his career, he decided to usurp his creator's authority over him. He was a powerful influence on other angels in heaven, who sided with him to overthrow Elohim. Due to his pride and arrogance, **he cast an eternal spell of refusal towards *God,*** but God used the same rejection to bound Lucifer into eternal destruction.

It was Lucifer's rejection of his righteous creator that destroyed his relationship and fellowship with Him. When Lucifer and the other angel accomplices decided to oppose and be disloyal to God, their purpose and position in the family of God were erase. *Ezekiel 28:13-17* and *Revelation 12:7-9 (KJV)* is an apparent reference to this statement.

# THE MISSION OF REJECTION

Lucifer also referred to as Satan or the devil, is the adversary of God and His people. **This adversary** is now roaming all over the earth seeking **to persuade all of humanity to reject**

**God's love** and instead, live and embrace rejection.

Satan uses every opportunity of **non-acceptance to attack people's emotions** so that he can influence them through deception into thinking that God doesn't care about them. **Satan manipulates people's minds into believing that God is their enemy, when, in fact, Satan is the chief offender, master manipulator and man's worse enemy**.

*Genesis 3 verses 1-6* demonstrate that Eve was the most powerful woman on earth. She was wise and possessed high self-esteem. Eve was the image of God, living in his likeness. **Satan plotted and attacked Eve by influencing her to disobey God and devalue herself.**

Through Satan's deception, Eve believed that he was encouraging her to rise from low self-esteem into a higher level of dignity and morale. Eve being deceived sadly misplaced her trust in Satan, found herself embracing good and evil and shackled to rejection and low self-esteem. When Eve and Adam became possessed by the power of rejection and low self-esteem, they became **fearful of God and hid from him.** *Genesis 3:8 (KJV).*

# DO NOT HIDE IN SELF-DEPRECIATION

Decide in your mind not to stay where rejection and low self- esteem have placed you. **It's time for you to exit the closet of fear. Come out from behind your tree of rejection, uproot your mindset from the ground of low self-esteem, and plant it into the soil of divine validation and appreciation of yourself to the glory of God.**

Low self-esteem is a **betrayal scale** of high- esteem, which the devil **created to deceive us into thinking negatively about ourselves.** If you don't maintain God's validation and appreciation of you, then your mind will become captivated by the devil, and other people's devaluation of you, **until you d**o.

Adam and Eve allowed the devil to **apprehend their thoughts and imaginations. Such incarceration of their mindset did not only depress them but also the entire human race**, as we do possess their nature. If you allow the ruin energy of rejection, and low self-esteem to control your emotions, then you will not be the only person who will be affected by the oppression thereof.

Everyone in your home, workplace, and wherever you are, will also be affected. Such a situation will continue to persist, until you **choose to stop comparing God's appreciation of you, with the devil's and others devaluation** of you. When others label you according to their perception, don't accept the *degrading analysis.*

## LOW SELF-ESTEEM DECONSTRUCTION AND MISSION

L ow self-esteem is birthed out of rejection. **LOW** Stand for *Less of Worth.* **SELF** signifies to *Steal Every Life Focus.* **ESTEEM** means to *Entrap Synergy Towards Enslaving Every Motivation.*

In low self-esteem operation, a person experiences feeling that make him/her feel less of their value.

The devil uses the influences of low self-esteem to steal

people's life focus, trapping the emotions that energize them to fellowship with others. He also uses such influences to captivate people's motivation and persuade them to decline all the appreciation of themselves.

## JESUS MADE A WAY TO ESCAPE ALL REJECTION

The devil thought that he could trap humanity forever in rejection, but Jesus Christ intervened, by way of his death, burial and Resurrection. Now all of humanity has access to release from the devil's bonds of rejection. The love of God is abundantly powerful against every shackle of rejection, fear and low self- esteem. That is the reason why the devil is working without ceasing, trying to influence all of humanity to reject God's love. Satan knows that if humanity accepts and embrace the love of God, that the power of God's love will cause his "ruin energy of rejection" to dissipate from our mindset.

## THE OPERATION AND RELATION OF REJECTION

Although rejection produces fear and low self-esteem, the devil will not function in those destructive emotions. He continually maintains boldness and high esteem of himself. But those who accept his rejection will immediately become a target, and the devil uses fear to eliminate their high regard and colonize their mindset to live as prisoners of low self-esteem.

Through his deceptive persuasion, the devil can keep people from identifying their divine validation. His mission is to keep a cap on people's potential and ability so that they will not fulfill God's purpose in their lives. The devil desires to keep humankind in subjection to him forever through his rejection influences. It is also the devil's will to dominate the minds of people through the hurt from rejection, and low self-esteem depressing feelings.

Rejection is the nurturer of unforgiveness, malice and bitterness. Therefore to overcome the mindset of those destructive characters be quick to forgive anyone who promotes the denial of you. Unforgiveness hinders togetherness; malice blocks communication and bitterness corrupt good fellowship.

## GUARDS OF REJECTION

Rejection is guarded safely by fear and low self-esteem. Those strong influential spirits are what the devil uses to target people's emotions and get them to condemn themselves, allowing him the ability to have total control over their lives. You are responsible for keeping a constant watch over your emotions. If you should encounter any abandonment feelings, use positive thoughts as a dehumidifier to remove all "fear moisture" of rejection from your emotion. Also, use the appreciation of yourself to cleanse all low self-esteem devaluation feelings from your mindset. If you choose not to uphold your mindset in the realm of steadfastness, then the symptoms of rejection will cause resentment and bitterness to fester in your emotions. Make it your duty to avoid situations that will compromise your self-esteem and expose you to rejection. Whenever you choose to agree with the feelings of rejection or low self-esteem, your conversations will become similar to your sentiments. If you're feeling good about yourself, then your communication will be entirely positive. However, if you allow low self-esteem to control your mindset, your conversation will naturally be negative.

Rejection can and will cause you to be perpetually judgmental of others. The disintegrating energy of rejection can cause people to be severely critical. It can also cause them to be unforgiving of both their own and others conduct. It can happen without the person who has been censorious being aware. **2 Samuel 12:1-14 (KJV)** reveals that King David was speedy in showing strong disapproval, of another man's conduct. In so doing, he quickly condemned the man to death when he had also committed a deplorable offence.

# THE DECONSTRUCTION OF REJECTION

**"R** E-" signifies ruin energy. "JEC-" is joint earning contract. "-TION" is the turmoil in one's nature.

The reverse order of the word "Rejection" is "NO-IT-CEJER." NOIT means "no offer interest transfer."

"C EJER" cancel every joint earning right." "Ruined energy" is when you are void of good feelings about yourself, and filled with negative, damaging feelings towards others. "Joint earning contract" speaks of rejection partnership and also signifies the symptoms of rejection that a person allows in their emotions. These symptoms are fear, discouragement, unbelief, disappointment, bitterness, anger, malice, unforgiveness, hate, resentment, hurt, murder, low self-esteem, depression, poverty and more. All of the symptoms mentioned above are characteristics that promote turmoil in one's nature.

It is mandatory that you cleanse your mind daily from all of the symptoms of rejection and renew your mindset with positive thoughts and imaginations. Failure to purge all the features of rejection from your emotions will cause you to enslave your mind into extreme brokenness.

It is very significant for one to know and understand that the rejection joint earning rights can only become inactive when you choose to reverse the rejection. When you reverse rejection, it signifies that you have decided to break the partnership with it and cancel all joint earning rights. Doing this will allow you to take back your emotions and your mindset from the captivity of rejection, fear and low self- esteem.

# KNOWING WHO IS THE SPIRIT OF REFUSAL

The devil is the spirit of rejection. I view him as a relationship and fellowship, destroying agent, and also a potential and ability limiter. When a person becomes captivated by the spirit of rejection, it will be evident that their relationship and fellowship with others will be "cross-threaded." That is due to mistrust, which causes the mind to change from a secure to an insecure mood periodically. This mood generates a lot of speculative feelings that regularly promotes inconclusive assumptions, which often creates contention among people and oneself.

# CROSS-THREADED RELATIONSHIPS

To fully explain a cross-threaded relationship, I will use the nut and bolt method. Whenever a nut is cross-threaded with a bolt, it becomes lopsided. To force it would then cause it to destroy the bolt and nut. Likewise, *if you allow rejection to force your mindset to be fearful and low self-esteem to cross-thread your emotions,* then your relationship and fellowship with God, yourself and others will become lopsided to the point where it can mentally, physically and emotionally damage you and others.

Such immense encounter can cause you to restrict your potentials and abilities to the place where you dilapidate them through neglect or misuse. In **1 Samuel 17:1-51 (KJV),** you will see that after hearing dismissal words from the captain of the Philistine's army, that low self-esteem, combined with the fear of rejection assisted King Saul to decline his self-worth and his ability as a warrior to win the battle against his Goliath. Goliath's intimidation tactics did not only captivate King Saul's mindset, but every soldier under his reign was also affected. All the fighting men of Israel and Judah became subjected to rejection; Goliath's words of fear tormented them for forty days. *1 Samuel 17:16* says twice per day for forty days, Goliath presented himself to disgrace King Saul and the army of Israel. *Verses 23-24* say that for forty days in both the morning and evening, Goliath came out against Israel to discredit them and for that same period; when the soldiers of the army of Israel saw Goliath, they fled from him. **Don't allow your Goliath of**

**rejection to humiliate you daily.** Embrace good courage, and refuse to permit the fear of rejection to block your abilities and potentials through low self-esteem. The fear of rejection will prevent you from doing great exploits throughout your lifetime. Decide not to run away like a coward from any trials. Tell yourself that you will not be weakened or broken by any Goliath of fear, rejection or low self-esteem. **Condition your mindset to terminate every insulting word that is aimed to sabotage your opportunity to excel in life. In verse 28 of 1 Samuel 17** tells us that Eliab, David's elder brother was firing dismissal words at David to turn him away from seeking information concerning the rewards, which King Saul promised to give to the warrior who killed Goliath!

*Sometimes people of status, even relatives and so-called friends, may scorn you because you don't seem to be as privileged.* You did not attain post-secondary education accreditation; do not possess a profitable paying job and may not have the worldly possessions or of the same socioeconomic status. Some relatives may even be embarrassed to be seen or associate with you because you just do not fit into their circle. Also, other people may not want you to excel but decline to focus your mind on those people **because they are** potential and ability **assassinators.**

**Do not allow anyone to devalue or terminate your worth.** David's elder brother saw him as a bush-boy, yard-boy, sheep watcher or in other words, a person who has no worth. Eliab assured in himself that David was not qualified to be or become a soldier in King Saul's army.

Eliab was privileged to be a soldier in King Saul's army, but he did not have any courage to defeat Goliath. He insulted

David and told him that he was only good enough to watch over the few sheep in his care. With a self-exalted mind and a wicked desire, Eliab further went on to chastise David and said to him that he had no business to leave the sheep in the wilderness and come to the battleground. **But what Eliab did not know is that man's reject was God's acceptance. Man's disability can become God's ability! Men look down on us while God uplifts us! Man's impossibility is God's possibility!**

*When scorned, you shouldn't invest in the contempt of anyone. If others regularly target you, it merely means that you are more advanced than they are.* You have abilities and potentials in ways that your mockers wish they could possess. When others, including yourself, perceive that no better is there for you to gain in life, you will always be a prisoner of rejection, fear and low self- esteem. **You need to decline such deposit from entering into the vault of your emotion. Stop feeling sorry for yourself, rise up and prove the enemy and yourself wrong,** by choosing to stand your ground against any Goliath situation that challenges your expectation for success. You might feel alone in combat with rejection struggles, but you are never standing alone. *God is present to help you,* through his grace; you will defeat your Goliath of anxiety, rejection, low self-esteem, depression and every failure. In **Verse 26 of 1 Samuel 17,** David presented himself for battle when it seemed all hope for Israel's victory was gone. David did not allow *Goliath's loudmouth to penetrate his positive feelings and intimidate him.* Such was because he knew that he possessed an extraordinary potential and was confident that he had the abilities of a mighty warrior to win the fight.

David was willing and prepared to challenge King Saul's

Goliath of rejection, fear and low self-esteem. In *1 Samuel 17:32-51* King Saul tried to persuade David to neglect his ability and potential by telling him that Goliath is a mighty warrior from his youth and pointed out the obvious that David had no fighting skills or experience. In respond, David advised King Saul that through God's help he had previously killed a lion and a bear and was confident that the same God of Israel that delivered him from the lion and bear would likewise protect and enable him to defeat Israel's Goliath of rejection and fear. **(Verses 38-39)** King Saul then gave David his armour of rejection, fear and low self-esteem, to wear into battle against his Goliath. But David expressed his disapproval of the armour and took them off. **Verse 40 of 1 Samuel 17** says David took his staff in his hand. The staff is the signification of courage, boldness and power. He went to the brook and took five stones from the stream. The brook represents the flow of the Holy Spirit. The five smooth stones represent God's unmerited favour, which is God's grace. So David removed Saul's armour of disgrace and put on God's *armour of* love, grace, good courage, boldness, and power. He used Christ the cornerstone of Israel, to knock down and slay Goliath. **Reference** *1 Samuel 17, verses 49-51.*

Like David, don't be afraid to challenge your Goliath of rejection, fear and low self-esteem. Don't listen to the voice of doubt that the devil will use to speak to you. *A voice that will tell you that you are not qualified* to challenge and conquer your Goliath of rejection and low self-esteem. Reject the armour of self-rejection, family rejection, children rejection, and husband or wife rejection. Put on God's boldness and high-esteem and step out to battle your Goliath of rejection and low self-esteem. With Jesus as your help, you cannot lose.

**Refuse to be a coward**, because you were born with the abilities and potentials for victory. God has appointed you to be a conservator over your emotions. You must preserve your thoughts and imaginations from the assaults of rejection, low self-esteem, fear and any other violations that are intended to impact your emotions negatively. **Failure to do so will cause you to conduct yourself in an obstructive way**.

Such responsibility is entirely personal. It's a task that only you can undertake. So don't depend on anyone else to assist you. Turn your sights on God, and place your expectation completely in his plan for you and **assure yourself that God will not fail you. He is going to see you through**. Also, you shall have victory over every rejection hurt that plague your life. You might say to yourself that you wish that you never have to deal with rejection, and that's so true. However, it's a battle that you cannot ignore, even though at times you feel like just giving up. I encourage you to hope in God, and you shall win **Big!!**

## REJECTION IS LIKE A CORRODED WICK IN A LAMP

If you operate through rejection feelings, then you will become like a lamp filled with oil and lit. But the brightness of it is decreased to dullness not because the fire needs fuel, and not because it needs a new shade or wick. No! The light of the lamp decreases because the shade is very dirty. However, such is not the source of the problem. The root cause is the dirty wick. The shade is continually getting sooty because the wick is corroded, and needs urgent cleaning. If you fail to acknowledge that the wick is corroded and needs to be clean, then it will cause the shade to get extremely dirty to the place where it only contributes very dull light.

Do you suffer from rejection, or often have your mindset sabotaged by refusal hurt, low self-esteem and fear? If yes, I want you to picture yourself as the previously mentioned lamp. The oil represents the institution of your emotions, which speaks of your feelings, behavioural responses, pleasure, and displeasure. Your emotional oil, which signifies your thoughts and imaginations, needs a clean-burning wick to reveal your emotions positively. The shade represents your mood. It is also the receiver and revealer of that which your ideas and creativity produce through your actions. My point is this; the physical oil lamp doesn't give efficient light. And it is continually making its shade dirty because the wick is loaded with debris and need cleaning.

In like manner, if you allow your thoughts and imaginations wick to become corroded with rejection, hurt, fear, low self- esteem, guilt, depression, resentment, bitterness, anger, disappointments, insecurity, loneliness, doubt, and isolation, then your emotion will produce these negative symptoms. As a result, those around you will see that you're getting dull, and your attitude towards them is getting worse. Also, it will be quite noticeable that your happiness light is rapidly changing from brightness to darkness.

Assess yourself and acknowledge that you need to cease from harmful behaviours. Take some time to clean the wicks of your thoughts and imaginations. In moving forward, you must be willing to clean up your emotional wick. By purging your mindset from every rejection fear, hurt, sadness, and low self-esteem degraded feelings. If not, you will continue to live in the bondage of rejection until you meet destruction. See yourself coming out of the captivity of rejection.

Decide in your mind to remove the dimmer switch that connects your emotions to rejection. You were born to shine, so shine! **Mathew 5:16 (NKJV)** says *to let your light so shine before men, that they may see your good works and glorify your Father in heaven.* Some days you will feel like shining is not possible, but look past such unable feeling, don't allow it to captivate your mindset. Encourage yourself into positive emotions. Doing so will enable you to rise above every influence of rejection and low self-esteem assignment, that is designed to trap you into hurt and resentment. You can become that which you think and feel, so choose a positive mindset at all times.

## FREEDOM FROM THE CORNS OF REJECTION

I once had two corns (calluses) on each of my toes except my big toes. The reason for these corns was the result of wearing shoes that were too tight regularly. After twenty-two years of not wearing any tight shoes, some of the corns dissipated, while other spots have minimal visibility. Rejection is like a tight pair of shoes; if you choose to wear such shoes, the corns of distress, frustration, resentment, bitterness, shame, anger, brokenness, unhappiness and low self-esteem, will squeeze your mindset for the length of time that you will be wearing them.

Those types of rejection "corns" are designed to afflict people with emotional pain and cause their positive mindset to deteriorate, to eradicate happiness and all of their aspirations. Although complete recovery from rejection hurt might take months or many years to heal, the moment you decide to stop wearing rejection, you will start to feel better. That feeling better will increase every day and night until you start realizing that some of the "corns" are no minimally visible or no longer visible.

Some wound spots may never disappear after healing; for such reason, tiny marks are often noticeable. Similarly, some scars of the pains of rejection and low self-esteem may stay with you until death. But you have to choose to decline their memories and don't allow them to distract you from appreciating yourself and accomplishing your goals. Don't permit your rejection experience to hold you in brokenness. Chose to ignore the spots of low self-esteem wound, and appreciate you always. Cease not to maintain positive thoughts towards yourself.

# HOW TO BREAK OUT FROM THE HURT OF REJECTION

Rejection is complicated, painful and destructive. The pains of rejection can cause one to become deeply depressed. It will also imprison your confidence if you authorize it to control your emotions. I believe that the most intense pain of rejection is within matters of love interest decline. **It is heartbreaking when you have strong feelings for someone, and you make**

**it known to that person, then your feelings are declined.**

Rejection cuts deep and will cause your emotions to experience excessive hurt through the torture of unforgiveness.

The pain of rejection will become applicable when you give your all into a relationship, only to be informed by that person whom you love, that he or she is not willing to reciprocate your feelings. It even hurts worse when said without any valid reason. **It can also cause you to experience sleepless nights; loss of appetite; weight gain; listless feelings in the home; at work or school; depression and isolation.** To access the pathway of wholesome healing, you must first understand the reasons for the particular rejection that you are experiencing. And get your deliverance from it and move forward with your life. **The love of God is the access code to unlock yourself from every hurt, pain and depressive state.** Should you ignore and dismiss the reasons for the rejections and fail to reverse the said refusal, then you will remain a prisoner of rejection. If you wish for peace of mind, then you need to surrender all of your desire unto God and use his words through prayer to give your mindset a daily catharsis.

Purging one's mind from all of the effects of rejection which is causing you to have emotional stress is extremely important.

# THE HURT OF VERBAL REJECTION

Verbal rejection is very detrimental to healthy communication. It can be extremely frustrating correcting a person who is struggling with verbal rejection. That person's emotions might be highly sensitive towards any manner of correction, especially if the instructions come from someone with whom they may have had a previous issue. Or someone who they just do not like! People who suffer from the pains of verbal rejection regularly perceive correction as an attempt to belittle them. Although in reality, the correction was meant to educate and build their self-worth.

Verbal rejection sufferers will find that their emotions are overly sensitive as they will automatically appear to become irritable and defensive. This sensitivity usually happens when anyone is trying to engage with them. People can experience verbal rejection anywhere such as in schools, workplaces, church, from marriage, friendship and at social gatherings.

The hurt and grief of Verbal Rejection will materialize when a person is excluded from conversations and decision making. The hurt of the exclusion can become very massive. It is my firm belief that the most painful verbal rejection occurrence takes place when people use unkind, hurtful, and insulting words to humiliate, scorn and devalue another human being.

The negative words of rejection that are intended to devalue someone are like seeds. If you become convinced that the harmful and destructive words are real, by so doing, you will give those words life, causing them to germinate in your mindset and grow daily in your feelings. **Those negative and harmful words are powerful, and if you allow them, they can affect and control your emotions; causing you to produce anger, resentment, bitterness, spitefulness, and continuous disrespect.**

**The tree of rejection must be cut down**; failure to destroy the tree of rejection **and root it out of your mindset** will allow it to develop more roots of hurt, fear, insecurity and unbelief in your life. The injury that one experience as a result of verbal rejection is the type of fuel that ignites low self-esteem. **With such fuel low self-esteem keeps its devaluation fire of the person burning in their feelings.** People, who allow rejection to mobilize their minds are operating under the influence of fear and will find it difficult to lower their guard and accept assistance from anyone.

*Until such persons make a conscious decision to withdraw their emotions from the decaying energy of the hurt of rejection, they will continue to mistrust and alienate the people who genuinely love and care about them.* If you allow the pain of rejection and its ruin energy to govern your feelings and dictate your conduct, then it is inevitable that such authorization, if not terminated, would destroy spousal relationships, friendships, work, and professional relationships and church fellowship. **Decide not to be a slave of verbal rejection.** Learn to ignore people's disdain words about you. What you don't receive will go from you.

# WHEN YOU DON'T UNDERSTAND

It is natural for us as human beings, to feel a sense of frustration when we do not comprehend specific issues that affect our lives. If you are experiencing rejection and do not have the answers that you are seeking, do not allow yourself to engage with resentment or other harmful and unproductive feelings. Otherwise, such emotions will only cause you to harbour ill feelings and perpetuate a life of dissatisfaction. You must reject any feelings that will cause you to feel or become irritated or exasperated. Learn to create a daily and nightly environment of positivity in your mindset.

**I encourage you to use wisdom and understanding at all times, bearing in mind that the devil desires to get you to surrender your control over your positive thoughts and imaginations. His goal is to sit on the Throne of your mindset. Also, it is for him to rule over your emotions, to abuse and blame you through the negativity that you may feel towards yourself and others.**

You may say that you have tried on numerous occasions to promote and foster a joyful mindset, but you still end up becoming depressed and irritable. Well, the reality is, brokenness does hurt, and disappointments will be inevitable until you come to an understanding that **you are not a product of errors.**

You must begin to prophesy positivity over your life. You came from perfectness, divine strength and favour. **Proverbs 18:21 states, "Death and life are in the power of the tongue: and they that love it shall eat the fruit thereof." (KJV).** You can use your tongue to either bless your life or curse it. **I, at this moment, prescribe that you operate your tongue to bless your life, rise from the slum of unproductive speaking over your life. Start to cultivate your mindset and sow seeds of good thinking into your emotions, so that you will reap the crops of progressiveness through positive interaction.** A section from *"Galatians 6:7 declares: "for whatsoever a man soweth, that shall he also reap."*

If you sow the persuasion seeds of the negativity of rejection and low self-esteem into your faculty of thinking, then **the** harmful effects of those seeds will navigate your emotion into the traffic of hurt. **It will also influence dysfunctionality in your inspiration and extreme confusion in your meditation.** With such thinking and feelings, your life will become subjected to depressing feelings. Motivate yourself daily **to think and act productively.** Do not encourage failure or limitation in what you **desire to achieve.**

## COMPREHENDING THE REASONS FOR REJECTION AND MOVING FORWARD

It is challenging to understand personal rejection when you have very little or no information why your biological parents, foster parents, siblings, relatives and friends may have abandoned you. When you find yourself in this scenario, you have to view the situation **as you would a puzzle which has a few pieces missing to complete it.** I would strongly suggest that you create those missing puzzle pieces and label them **"no longer required!"** Use the no longer required as the key in closing that aspect of your life. It is imperative that you have a clear understanding of the fact, that there will be events in your life that you may never obtain the answers that you seek, regardless of how hard you may try to get that information.

**Resist the urge** to seek out unprofitable information that will only increase your level of frustration, hurt and disappointment. Such negativity will only create tremendous amounts of emptiness in your life. Find your **"peace in God."** Close this chapter of your life and be determined not to open it for the remainder of your lifespan. In *John 14:27, Christ* says, "**Peace I**

leave with you, my peace I give unto you: not as the world giveth, give I unto you. Let not your heart be troubled, neither let it be afraid." (KJV).

Do not at any time allow unhappiness, which is a deficit of understanding, to rule over your ability to rise and fulfill **the purpose for which you came into this world**. Regardless of what anyone may say to you, you are not "**an accident!**" Your entry into this world signifies that you were destined to **BE!** Many did not make it *to conception*, but you did. **You escaped abortion and still-birth**. You overcame darkness and saw the light of life. So don't allow the confusion of the assignment of rejection against your emotions, to imprison your mindset.

## DESIRE TO ABIDE IN HAPPINESS

**R**ejection is a destroyer of happiness, but there is a happiness that is not immune to such a destructive force. There are two states of happiness. *Self-created happiness* and *Spiritual happiness.* Self-created happiness is obtained when your bills are paid off; you're taken to dinner, to watch a movie, go on vacation, given a gift of your liking, or whenever you get treated in a fashion that makes you feel appreciated.

Self-created happiness seems very delightful because everything is undertaken and completed according to your desire. **However, such pleasures can be destructive**, because when the person who created the atmosphere that caused you to feel happy, ceases to provide those pleasures, **it can leave you with anger, resentment, irritability, mistrust, annoyance, fear, heartache, loneliness and brokenness.** Spiritual happiness, which is divine, is the only true happiness. **No person or thing can give you this type of joy.**

Spiritual happiness hormone was designed in your soul by the Most High God, Our Creator. It can only become activated by your faith in God and sincere obedience to his word. No one or anything can take this happiness from you. The only person with the power to make this happiness dormant in you is YOU. When you have spiritual happiness, and someone provides self-created happiness, then decides to withdraw these desirables, **you will still be happy, peaceful and content**.

Knowing it was not self-created happiness that was sustaining you, it was God's perfect happiness. **Seek to rely on the happiness of God**. He is the only one who can provide true happiness. Renounce rejection claim on your joyfulness and oppose depression invasion on your mindset. Making yourself unhappy and living in such misery is a total waste of energy and is not beneficial in any manner. **Don't evaluate your potentials and abilities through the negative lens of unhappiness. There is no gain when you invest in sadness**. Make a conscious decision to be happy and emancipate your mindset from the bondage of sorrow.

Refuse to engage with the inner conflicts and pain of rejection. Embrace the power of understanding and appreciation. Believe that you are an extraordinary masterpiece and unique in every way. Cease not to encourage yourself with the confidence that in spite of every setback and failure you have experienced from your past to present, you are still a worthy person. In doing so, you will indeed start being grateful, and extremely thankful that you are worthy of living a loving, peaceful and joyful life.

**Joyfulness is a complete feeling of peace and whole-someness from God.** The joy of God that believers possess through the Holy Spirit **is not subject to any pain, suffering, weaknesses or problematic circumstances.** The Apostle Paul encouraged the Philippians believers to have complete joy in the Lord **(Phi 4:4).** He testified to the Corinthian believers that for him to remain at the right level in Christ so that pride would not take over his heart and captivate his pleasure for Christ, that it was for such a reason the Lord allowed Satan to afflict him with a thorn in his flesh. Paul then, on three occasions through prayers, asked God to deliver him from the thorn, but God did not. God told him, **"My unmerited favour is sufficient for you and my strength is made perfect in weakness."** *(KJV) 2 Cor12:7-9.*

Paul refused to allow infirmities to steal away his joy in Christ, so in sickness, he joyfully glorifies God through Christ. Although Christ refused to deliver Paul from the thorn in his flesh, Paul joyfully confessed in *Phil 1:21 (KJV) "that for him to live is Christ."* He did not seek the joy of the flesh, because such happiness is only temporary and leads into sorrows, and such grief is the key to open up the destruction to one's soul. But the joy of the Spirit is permanent and leads to victory over trials. *"The joy of the Lord is the believer's strength," says Neh 8:10.*

There are no demons or any trials that can break the power of the Lord that the believers receive through the Holy Spirit. Paul and Silas were beaten on their backs until they were bruised and bloody. Shackled in chains, cast into prison, but in spite of the pain and suffering that they endured, they joyfully prayed and sang to worship God, through His Holy Spirit.

Reference *Acts 16: 23-25 (KJV).*

People of **faith are not servants of a depressed or a weak mindset**, and we should not engage in or perpetuate the negative spirits of sorrow or weakness. *Your joy must stay within you regardless of whatsoever trials you may encounter* in life because the Lord is our defender. *Psalms 5:11 (KJV).* Although King David experienced significant amounts of tests and pain in his life, he continuously encouraged himself by stating, *"I will be happy and joyful in the Lord, I will sing praise unto Him." (Psalms 9:2 KJV). Also, Psalms 16:11* tells us that David was a man who had absolute confidence in God. He was fully persuaded knowing that God would show him the way of life. It is of such conviction that he encouraged us, that with the presence of God in our lives, we will experience sufficient joy. He testified that in the power of God, there are pleasures forever.

There is a happiness hormone sensor in our mindset that I call, peace or tranquillity. *This hormone is similar to oxygen.* Our lungs need oxygen for us to breathe, and it is transported to the entire body through our red blood cells for the production of energy. When a human being experiences oxygen deficiency, the body would enter into a weakened state. Furthermore, if the interference is not quickly and effectively corrected, then it would result in a loss of life. (Science Net Links).

Similarly, *our mindset requires peace to stabilize our emotions in order, to create a state of contentment.* When our thoughts and imaginations are fuelled by satisfaction, it causes us to become energized with positive motivation. However, when our feelings experience a deficiency of peace, **it weakens our mindset and produces negative emotions**, which translate into unhappiness and failure. **If you should find yourself attached to negative and sorrowful feelings, you need to detach your mindset from such unprofitable connection immediately.**

Failure to decline the interaction would cause you to become a prisoner of brokenness in subjection to feelings of torment and confusion. Our mindset was not designed by God to function through rejection's negative energy; it was fashioned to operate by positive force. I will use a car battery as an example. If you seek to join the negative to the positive, it would short circuit the battery and cause total damage or severe charging problems. In like manner, **if you connect the negative feelings of rejection to your positive thinking, you will short circuit your emotion and damage your cells of positive energy** to the place where your mindset is no longer maintains peace or any happiness charge.

## DON'T CONCEAL YOURSELF IN FEAR OF REJECTION

I highly recommend that at all times, you be aware and **be extra cautious in not using the fear rejection as a defence mechanism to conceal yourself.** It's possible to use the ruin energy of rejection and low self-esteem to build a protective wall around yourself. And while being heavily guarded by brokenness, you are deceived by fear which convinces you into believing that you are secure, untouchable and unmovable.

Due to such misconception, you are entirely influenced to think that no one will ever be able to penetrate your maximum protective care. Or cause you pain and grief ever again. **But the truth is, you are completely unprotected and therefore, vulnerable to every target from rejection. To prevent rejection, you must breakdown your walls of its fear, unlock every gate of its hurt, with the appreciation of yourself and put down your fake sword of counterfeit victory.**

## YOU CANNOT PRETEND TO DEFEAT THE FEAR OF REJECTION

Stop! No more pretending to be stronger than the pains of rejection because, in pretence mood, you will always lose.

**Stop using fear, and unproductive feelings to motivate you into moving forward.** To gain real victory, you have to train your thoughts and imaginations into producing a healthy mindset of courageous thinking. **Then use that bold mindset to combat all the concepts of rejection.**

## BE ALERT AGAINST THE DECEPTION OF THE FEAR OF REJECTION

The fear of rejection, along with its associated depressing feelings, will psychologically deceive you into thinking that you are progressing and getting much better. **When in truth, you are in a state of stagnation.** The fear of rejection will 'create a false sense of illusion which will cause you to believe that you are advancing mentally, when, in fact, you have not progressed.

Believe wholeheartedly in God's love, and the fear of rejection will fail. The torment that rejection fear generates can cause a person to stand down and accept defeat. Decline to surrender! Like a well-trained soldier prepared for war, in like manner learn the cycle and pattern of rejection and low self-esteem. So that when they rear their ugly heads and come at you like roaring lions, you will be prepared and ready to counteract their attack. Be determined to battle against the fear of rejection and low self-esteem until its influences are entirely defeated in your emotion.

Refuse to labour in the hurt of rejection and low self-esteem. **Don't use fear as your shelter from your storm of rejection**. Learn to transfer your mind from fear to complete love. Otherwise, fear will cause you to remain in the torment of rejection and the self-pithiness of low self-esteem. Believe in love completely! Why should you? Because perfect love has the power to remove fear out of your thoughts and imaginations, which would allow you to be, free to accomplish your God-given goals. *1 John 4:18 (KJV)*. *…..perfect love casteth out fear*: **because of fear hath torment.**

## DON'T TURN ONTO THE EXIT OF REJECTION

Rejection is a pathway that takes you into self-devaluation. That is the place where you allow people's harmful perception of you to trap you. It is where the fear of rejection becomes your security, and worthless feelings become your advisor. Also, it is where low self-esteem "plagues" your abilities and potentials, influencing your mindset through thoughts of deception. Those deceptive thoughts will make you believe that you are only a failure, not suitable for anything and do not possess any self-worth. You may even think that you would never get married because you're too ugly or not pretty/handsome enough. You may also believe you will never be a good mother or father, wife or husband.

Rejection can make you think and feel as if you cannot trust another person ever. That you are incapable of loving anyone, that another person could not love you in return. To them, it seems you do not possess the qualities or abilities to love or be loved. That you are unworthy of a happy and satisfying marriage, and you are not capable of undertaking and accomplishing goals in your life. Such as returning to school; completing the education that you had failed to finish earlier in life; excelling to a higher level of education or attaining a superior quality of life other than the low standard that you may be currently living.

**Rejection can also cause you to second guess yourself.** The devil will make you think that whatever you truly desire in life is unattainable because you are not good enough to obtain it. The devil is the master and orchestrator of lies. **Do not embrace his deceptive persuasion.** You can do all things through Christ's strength given unto you. (*Phi 4:13 KJV*). Whatsoever you believe to happen will be, if you do not doubt in your desire that which you declare and hope to see. If you communicate with God and request of him any particular thing, you must rely on him to supply your petition. Knowing you indeed shall get what you desire of him. *Mark 11:23-24 (KJV)*

If you should ever find yourself on the Pathway of Rejection, you need to exit and get onto *Progress Street.* Going in this direction will lead you into self-evaluation. **Progress Street is where you recognize who you are**, and believe that you are exceptional, beautiful or handsome, virtuous and full of excellence and integrity. Furthermore, this is where you acknowledge your God-given purpose and embrace your abilities and potentials. **The street of progress will cause you to excel exclusively and exceedingly**. Above all, the negative voices that are designed and appointed to mentally, physically and emotionally bind you in low self-esteem, rejection, hurt and fear. The decision is yours to make, not your opposers. Ask God to help you make the correct decision.

# YOU ARE NOT A PRISONER OF REJECTION

Rejection and stress have the influences to contribute excess burden to one's health. They can work through people's emotions, to impact and transform our **mindset from positive to negative**. Although difficult and challenging, you must refuse to become addicted or enslaved by any dysfunctional behaviour. You are definitely not a prisoner of rejection and its depressing symptoms.

You can overcome verbal, spousal, self-rejection, children, siblings, relatives, friends, or whatever other rejections that you may be experiencing. In the book of *1 Samuel, chapter 1 and 2 (KJV),* you will see as I illustrate that Hannah defeated all the influences of rejection that challenged her emotions. It is evident in the text that Peninnah, who was able to have children, saw herself as "complete." On the other hand, Hannah's purpose was to have a son, but she was barren. However, her faith in God was unwavering, so she ceased not to consult God through her prayers desiring of him to bless her to conceive.

I'm of the understanding that Peninnah viewed Hannah's daily petitions to God as a failure and continually mocked her. Peninnah thought that Hannah would never be able to have a baby and was going to die barren. She felt that God would not bless Hannah with the son that she so desires to give Elkanah. Peninnah was convinced that even though Elkanah loved Hannah. She was still nothing but a woman of voidness. But she Peninnah is very fruitful in childbearing, and that is what makes her womb a blessing. On the other hand, Hannah is perceived as nothing but a barren woman. Due to the constant harassment and verbal abuse, Hannah became angry and bitter. Daily and nightly, she has to battle against the effects of rejection fear, hurt, sorrows, discouragement, disappointments and confusion, of such was the conflict that pushed her into a state of depression.

However, throughout Hannah's pain and turmoil, Hannah was determined to endure and trust God ultimately. Her mind was made up to fight a good fight of faith. Even though her many days and nights of prayers seem not to effect God's ears, Hannah refused to stop seeking God for her breakthrough. She did not allow the many years of Peninnah's verbal abuse and rejection to enslave her emotions. Even though Elkanah loved her more, Hannah still could not see herself without the son that her heart desired. Elkanah tried to comfort Hannah to get her to realize that although she has not given him any sons, he loved her. Also, his love was worth much more than ten sons.

In the biblical world, (10) signifies testimony, law, responsibility and the completeness of order.

(Biblestudy.org). Ten sons would, therefore, have been a "perfect family," something any woman in that generation would have desired.

Hannah's afflictions did not cause her to seek deliverance in her husband. It drove her closer to God and motivated her to depend upon him to provide her needs entirely. Hannah desired to have a "God purpose baby." She refused to allow herself to become a prisoner of rejection or low self-esteem; she used her confidence in God to oppose every assignment of reproach and depression. She promised God that if He blessed her with a baby boy, she would bestow her son back to him all the days of his life. *(1SA 1:9-11 KJV)*.

Hannah's humility has impacted my life tremendously. In her quest to reach out to God for victory over her barrenness, Hannah was accused falsely by a man of God. A highly regarded high priest whose name was Eli. While praying in the temple, Eli viewed Hannah's method of praying to God as strange because she was praying inwardly and displayed an outward action that mimicked someone who was severely intoxicated. Hannah felt rejected, isolated, and her spirit was in deep sorrow as a result of Peninnah's constant torment, compounded with Eli's false accusations. **But in spite of her opponent's hurtful behaviours, Hannah refused to allow Peninnah's, Eli's or anyone else's hurtful words and false accusations to prevent her from holding on to God's grace.**

Hannah's name means "grace," which signifies that she had favour. Hannah was determined entirely to uproot and cast down every feeling of disgrace from her mindset. Although

Hannah was hurting, she did not get angry at Eli, nor did she depart from the temple and criticize him or his ministry. In spite, he had made inaccurate painful accusations against her. Hannah humbly and respectfully responded to Eli's criticism by stating, "Master, I am a woman of depression. I have not drunk either unfermented wine or fermented. However, my soul is drunk with sorrow, so what you saw was an outpouring of my pains unto the Lord Jehovah. So do not see me as a daughter of Belial, do not view me as a worth-less woman, as a wicked woman, or as an unrighteous woman, because I am not."

Hannah's humble appeal to Eli, the man of God, caused him to release her to go in peace. Eli prayed Jehovah would give her what she desired. Hannah was happy that she had given all of her burdens to God. She had willingly surrendered all to God, and in doing so, she was set free from verbal abuse, oppression, depression, disappointments, fear and even the hurt of refusal.

*1 Samuel 1:12-19. (KJV)* *helps us to conclude* that was the year of victory over Peninnah's rejection and success over bareness. It was the year of fruitfulness. Hannah was able to conceive and gave birth to a God purposed baby boy.

It is truly gratifying to know that even when God allows us to go through tests and challenging times, the result is that we will become what He has ordained us to be. Hannah desired to have one son, but God blessed her with three sons and two daughters, *1 SA 2:20-21.* Five is the number of grace and is equivalent to divine favour. Through reviewing this particular scripture, I realized Peninnah's rejection of Hannah was needed to motivate Hannah and draw her closer to God. Once you genuinely seek God, He will reverse all manner of barrenness from your life. **When you are going through an awkward situation, you may think that there is no hope that you cannot succeed. But I encourage you not to allow your circumstances to manipulate your mindset into believing that you are a captive of whatsoever your hindrances might be.**

If you are persistent like Hannah and embrace hope and trust in God even when the situation does not look possible, God will break your chains of rejection. Also, He will do the same for you, as he did for Hannah. Investing sincere faith in God means that He will favour you and grant your desires, at his appointed time. Refuse to deposit your faith into other people's rejection of you and make up your mind to never surrender to hopelessness.

## DO NOT LET REJECTION BECOME A STANDARD IN YOUR LIFE

If you are chained in the pit of rejection with low self-esteem, after a while, it can become routine for you to decide not to take the option out of such a negative mindset. It can occur if you allow your hormones which are attached to positive thinking, to become subservient to hopelessness. The pit of rejection is your battlefield. Your challenger is low self-esteem, but you cannot defeat low self-esteem on the battlefield of rejection if you don't understand its source of power. The power of low self-esteem is not unbreakable or unmovable like it has tried to influence and persuade our minds into believing. **The power of rejection and low self-esteem is fuelled by unbelief, and** the input cable that keeps your thoughts and imaginations connected to rejection and low self-esteem is called fear. So chose not to yoke your feelings with fear.

# NEVER GIVE IN TO THE VOICE OF REJECTION

The voice of rejection and low self-esteem is mentally influencing, but you can and will overcome it if you choose to cease from listening to its counsel. Always resist communicating with rejection or low self-esteem and at no time, allow your emotions to justify its reasoning.

**It is the will of the devil to use fear and low self-esteem to persuade your mindset into viewing yourself with disgust and hatred.** It is also his purpose to negatively affect your life and propel you into a life-long pattern of unproductivity. Do not allow the devil to have such authority over you.

You possess authority through the love of Christ to revoke and nullify rejection, low self-esteem, depression, fear, doubt, resentment and all other works of the enemy in and out of your life. "*Behold I have given you the power to tread on serpents and scorpions and over the power of the enemy and nothing shall by any means hurt you.*"(*Luke 10:19 KJV*) The hurt of rejection and the unprogressive feelings of low self-esteem can only hurt you if you fail to keep the power of Christ active in your mindset.

If you focus your mind on your past or present circumstances, then every target that the devil intends to affect you will penetrate your emotion and injure your ability to interact.

## DON'T ALLOW YOUR LIFE TO BE ATTRACTED TO FEAR OR REJECTION

**F**ear is a spirit that is entirely shielded by deception. It aims to get someone to become fully persuaded into an agreement with its assignment. **Fear requires that its prey direct all attention to its intimidation schemes. Because, when anyone becomes timid and subjected to such cowardness, it automatically enables them to engage in failure. Which causes a person to become subjected to lack of success, chose not to normalize fear in your life.** Decline the influence of fear and rejection, and refrain your mindset from attending to its ruin feelings.

**Whatever you authorize to capture your attention will precisely become your attraction.** Such captivation can lead to negative relation, and such connection will open your mind to distraction, and distraction produces affliction and affliction leads to persecution. Avoid persecuting yourself with the fearful and ruin energy of rejection's sentiment and unhappiness. Forbid all ideas that are intended for you, to justify any hurt of refusal in your life. Failure to do so will cause you to remain bound to the ruin energy of rejection. **If you don't know what you deserve, then you will continue to attach yourself to what you must give up.** You are worthy of a happy life, so start to promote appreciation of yourself in your daily lifestyle.

To invest in any form of rejection will only contribute brokenness interest in your emotions. Also, to withdraw feelings from such an account will, in turn, bankrupt your mindset towards yourself and others.

## GET OUT OF YOUR UNHEALTHY MARRIAGE- DO NOT STAY BECAUSE OF FEAR

To assist you in comprehending my point of view on the above topic; I will use an analogy to solidify my perspective.

Say you are married, and your relationship is severely dysfunctional. It is plagued with frustration, contention, discouragement, discomfort, anger, disappointments, bitterness, malice, unforgiveness, hate and unhappiness. However, you speak with your spouse about obtaining counselling to address the issues, but your spouse does not see any need for advice concerning the union. Nevertheless, spouse insists that you remain married in spite of the fact both parties are very unhappy and miserable together.

That spouse who is in denial is likening to an apple tree in a desert. It is a reality that God did not design a desert to grow apple trees because of its arid conditions. So, if you should choose to plant one there, then you will be overworking yourself by watering it so that it may develop. And despite all the watering, you realize that it will be almost impossible, for the apple tree will not grow in such a dry or arid condition. You are still committed to being persistent in watering it. Likewise, you know that you should stop pouring out your energy to that "desert" husband or wife. However, because you are entirely convinced that your love for him or her will cause the relationship to grow into the marriage that you desire. You continue to water and provide the love and care that is needed. **But you need to accept the truth which is this: regardless of your good intentions unless the spouse is committed and willing to adjust and make the necessary changes, all of your hard work and love will only be in vain.**

Faith in those types of relationships is not practical or realistic. **Expectations must be connected to the will of God, in conjunction with wisdom, knowledge and understanding, to prevent any hopes of confusion and wasted years.** You can spend years investing your time, gifts and talents in the wrong places, in the wrong people and also in inappropriate relationships. And after five, ten, fifteen or twenty years of marriage, you realize that it doesn't make sense. **It was all a waste of your value.**

**No one will give up what they don't purpose to let go.** Therefore, some people would prefer to die before making changes to improve and enhance their relationship with their spouses. A **lifetime with a person that is not willing to adjust for the better will be nothing but frustration, hurt and grief. God does not approve such types of relationships and conduct.**

Some wives and husbands know that their marriages are a desert, and their relationship with each other is like the previously mentioned, apple tree. However, due to the fact they have spent so many years investing in what I call, "we don't agree together," they exist in an uncooperative relationship. These spouses allow themselves to remain trapped in a lifetime pattern of fear, rejection and low self-esteem. Even though it becomes very transparent that it is not the will of God for people who are living in loveless marriages to remain in such divided, unhappy and unhealthy lifestyles. The fear of starting over will supersede the logic of bringing the relationship to an end.

Spouses can pour out all the potentials that they have into their spousal relationships, but if a spouse partially or wholly rejects the other spouse, then the level of love and submission that is mandatory to establish excellent communication, respect and comfort will be shallow.

**Respect is what every husband seeks. Love and comfort are the desires of every wife. If a wife rejects her husband or if the husband rejects his wife to a certain extent, the level of honour and love for each other will start to diminish.** A wife who functions in rejection and low self-esteem modes will find it very difficult to submit to her husband. In such a fashion, the wife is operating in the realm of fear, mistrust, and insecurity. Her emotions are fired up by ruin energy. The husband will not be able to love his wife like Christ loves the church if he also operates in the modes of rejection and low self-esteem.

Functioning in these styles opposes the unity that produces and binds a healthy, loving relationship. Amos 3:3 (KJV) says, *"Can two people walk together without agreeing on the direction?"* No! Where there is no agreement, contention will never cease and where contention rules, division labours to produce unfaithfulness and termination of the relationship.

Rejection in marriage is tremendously unhealthy. It hinders good fellowship in the relationship. Many marriages have and still are collapsing into divorce due to the fear of rejection and the devaluation feelings of low self-esteem, which has been the root cause of the disintegration and depreciation of marriages over the ages. **If you choose not to give up your negative life-styles and pattern of behaviour, then you should not enter into any form of relationship with any person who is determined to live in a positive mindset, because such partnerships will not be happy or prosperous.**

## MOTHERS' REASONS FOR REJECTION

Some mothers willingly reject their child/ren. They may feel that they are too immature, inexperienced and perhaps terrified to raise a child alone. They may lack the support of shared responsibility from the biological father or a responsible adult. Other mothers are pressured and forced by family members into undertaking the act of rejection (having their child/ren adopted) because they do not wish to be scorned by the community due to the child/ren being born illegitimately.

Some mothers have rejected their child/ren because they believe parenting a baby would be inconvenient and conflict with their carefree lifestyles. Those could be the mothers who are incapable or unwilling to take responsibility for their actions. They too might not have been shown genuine love by their own mothers, therefore they have no concept of love. Also, some mothers reject their child/ren because they recognize that there is someone else who would do a better job of parenting than they would. Surprisingly, there are men and women who after being rejected by their birth mothers, went into foster care, or were privately adopted, were cared for in a happy and loving home.

However, because of the adoption, many were able to achieve superior levels of education, social amenities, employment, success, and comfortable living. That had they stayed with their birth parent(s) they probably would not experience how parents' rejection feels. But they would have suffered potential and abilities lost, and they would not have been as happy or prosperous.

## UNDERSTANDING PARENTAL REJECTION

As we have already established, rejection is hugely destructive to the human psyche and parental neglect and abandonment, I believe, is viewed to be the worst component of rejection. While parental rejection is extensively devastating and generates continuous emotional hurt, I intend to cover this sensitive topic with respect and empathy towards the parents who for whatever reasons, rejected their children. A large population of people, regardless of where in the world they were born or raised, were parented by a mother or father figure other than their birth-mother or biological father. In some cultures, children only knew one parent, which was the mother, as many fathers shirked their responsibilities.

To better their lives and the lives of their children, women have left their countries of birth, migrated to foreign countries, primarily North America and the United Kingdom. Countries where the standard of living and employment opportunities are at a higher advantage. Many children were therefore left in the care of family members such as grandmothers, aunts or another guardian, and in many cases these children did not receive the proper care that they deserved. Even though some mothers created new lives for themselves in these foreign countries, the children they left behind were not included in that new life.

Some children were loved and received tender loving care, while others received just the opposite. Far too many vulnerable children were abused and taken advantage of by family members before they were able to reunite and reintegrate with their biological mothers. A large portion of children grew into adults in abusive homes and became the product of a cycle of abuse. In fewer cases, some children were privately adopted and were raised in safe and happy homes by people who loved and cared for them.

It's a possibility that you were loved, and treated the best by your adopted parent or parents, but you always felt like something was still missing from your life. You can't explain it, but deep down inside, at times you have to deal with that personal inner conflict. It is also possible that you were not treated well by your adopted parent or parents, and you are so desperate for the answers to your why? But it seems as if they will never materialize. It can take years for you to get some answers, but some you may never understand or accomplish.

It took Moses forty years to acquire the solution for his inner conflict. At three months old, he was rejected by his parents, but that act of rejection was undertaken to preserve Moses' life. In the period when Moses was born, the ruling Pharaoh's mission was to dehumanize Jacob's descendants and expunge the generations of Israel because he feared their abilities and potentials. To accomplish his plan, Pharaoh issued a decree which stated all the female babies born to Hebrew women must be kept alive, but all male babies must be thrown into the river to perish. *Exodus 1:6-22 (KJV)*.

Moses' mother realized that she had two choices; one was to keep her son, and they would die together or to reject her son and hope that he will survive the rejection. While many other mothers obeyed the decree, rejected and cast their baby boys into the river to die out of fear, Moses' mother did not comply with the order. Instead, she lovingly and wisely secured her son in a floating vessel, with the faith and belief that someone would rescue, adopt and love him.

The depth of a mother's faith is unpredictable and unmeasurable. One can only imagine that it was an arduous and heartbreaking process for Moses' mother to place and watch her three-month-old baby floating down the stream, knowing that there was a possibility that he could drown, be devoured by a wild animal or die of hunger before someone with a caring and loving heart found him. That was a risk she was willing to take to save her baby.

As wrong as it might seem and as hurtful as it might feel, I applaud Moses' mother for her actions. Where there is life, there is hope! That wonderful mother's idea was risky, but it certainly ended well. Ironically, it was Pharaoh's daughter who saw and rescued Moses while she was in the river taking a bath. Again the favour of God was upon Moses because it was his birth-mother who was sought when Pharaoh's daughter needed a wet-nurse to feed him.

Moses was privileged to receive breastfeeding by his birth-mother, although Pharaoh's daughter was unaware of this fact. Moses' mother was blessed to have had a second opportunity to spend some more precious time with her son until he was weaned. It must have been complicated to give her son up a second time, but she knew that she had made the right decision to keep her son alive. (*Exodus 2:1-15 KJV*).

# SURVIVING REJECTION

The reason for your encounters of rejection might not make sense to you. It may have caused you to experience years of bitterness and emotional pain. However, the outlook that you should have at this point in your life should be like the story of Moses. You survived rejection! Many died, but thank God you were not one of the statistics. Conclusively, the destructive element of the termination order against your life failed, *because you were destined to overcome*. With that significant victory, you can choose to stand down in disappointments, fears, brokenness, regret, anger and unforgiveness and all other facets of rejection, but such a move will be catastrophic.

There is another choice on the table. You can resist and decline that destructive path, and climb out of the pit of your rejection. Embrace the life that God has designed for you. The choice is only yours to decide!

Moses learnt that he was not an Egyptian and with that knowledge, he utilized all the resources that were needed for him to succeed. When life is sweet, you have to learn how to sustain yourself in the sweetness of it. When it gets bitter, that is when you find the courage to go through the storms, not allowing challenges to keep you from the lifetime goal of sweetness. *"There shall not any man be able to stand before thee all the days of thy life: as I was with Moses, so I will be with thee: I will not fail thee, nor forsake thee"* says *Joshua 1:5 (KJV).*

Moses willingness to search out his origin and embrace his true identity landed him into serious problems. He killed an Egyptian man to protect his Israelite brother with the expectation that his brother would accept him as a fellow Israelite, but he was rejected.

The killing of the Egyptian caused the Pharaoh's family that adopted, raised and loved him from three months old, and provided him with all the wealth and comfort that Egypt had to offer, to despise and reject him at the age of forty. This incident became the second time that Moses went through rejection.

Perhaps you can relate to Moses' unfortunate experience, where you are viewed as the enemy and shunned by your adopted family, friends and society. But bear in mind that man's reject can become God's project. God will use that time of crisis in your life to show forth his power and bring you into his purpose. *Psalm 27:10 (KJV) declares, "When my father and my mother forsake me, then the LORD will take me up"*

Moses' rejection by his foster parents was a perfect opportunity for the Lord to elevate him out of the hurt of rejection, disappointment, fear and low self-esteem. God specializes in delivering people from all types of refusal. He rescued Moses and used him to showcase his excellence in the entire land of Egypt. If your rejection is similar to that of Moses, then the Lord can and will do the same for you. Will you trust him to help you?

# REJECTION IN AND OUT OF THE WOMB

There are many mothers in this world who upon discovering that they are pregnant, fearfully reject the child that they are carrying through abortion. Also, they are mothers who give birth, then deny the child into death. Such dismissals may occur due to the fear of rejection from the male partners, family members, friends or the general public. If your mother gave birth to you, but declined you by leaving you at the hospital; in a washroom; on the sidewalk; on a bus; in a car; in some bush; in a field; on the beach; by the riverside; in a cemetery; with a total stranger; with a friend or family members, you should be thankful. Even though you have to grow, not knowing her, and having her guidance, she allowed you to stay alive. She could have rejected you into death, but like Moses' mother, she chose to reject you into life, hoping that you say alive and prosper.

You might say it would have been better if she had terminated your life because you have lived a complicated and challenging experience and do not see any value in living. It might also be your opinion that if your mother was in your life, you might have had a better life. That may be a fair statement to make, but it can also be seen as unjustifiable speculation. For it's a possibility that if you were with her, you would have been worse. So even though you may have grown into an adult without knowing the identity of your mother, take comfort in knowing that, like Moses' mother who gently positioned him into a water basket and placed him in the river to be discovered, your mother may have undertaken a similar action, which saved your life. Celebrate your life and give God thanks for He has a purpose for you. **1 *Thessalonians 5:18 (NKJV)*** says, ***"In*** *everything give thanks, for this is the will of God in Christ Jesus for you."* As human beings, it is natural for us to think that some of these women's actions are deplorable and punishable. But only God entirely knows the intent of every hearts. Therefore, it is significant that we be willing to forgive in all circumstances. While the Lord Jesus was on the cross experiencing every manner of rejection, He uttered these words, *"Father forgive them for they know not what they do." Luke 23:34. (KJV)*

# MY EXPERIENCE OF REJECTION

I resented my mother for many years and was furious and bitter towards her. I was suffering with what I called "void of a mother's love and attention." I had no memories of a loving relationship with my mother. I was longing to hear my mother express maternal affection for me. I desperately wanted a motherly hug and have her as that person to whom I could relate like a best friend. To hear my mother utter a simple "I love you," would have been sufficient for me.

My desire for my mother's love was so intense that when my older daughter was three years old, I pretended that she was my mother. I would let her walk me to the door, hug me and kiss me goodbye. I searched for that mother's love and affection for many years in multiple relationships with women, but all I ended up with was a life of emptiness.

One day I saw my mother and was extremely happy to see her, and as I moved forward to give her a big hug, she pushed me away from her with a powerful force that I did not Expect.

My eyes immediately flooded with tears due to her rejection. After that very public episode of rejection, I decided in my mind that my mother was dead to me and whenever anyone inquired about my mother, I would respond by stating that she had gone home, meaning that she had passed away.

Blocking my mother out of my mind did not quite successfully make the void go away because every year on Mother's Day, when I hear other people speaking about their mother, I would wish like every normal human being, that I could visit and spend some time with her, talking and laughing around the dining table.

That void was vacated when I completely surrendered my life and all my heart's desires to Christ Jesus. I asked the Lord to remove all of the rejection bitterness, and hurt from within my heart, that I was feeling towards my mother and replaced it with his love. Also, to forgive me of despising her, and to forgive her, for the rejection that she displayed towards me.

After God did that excellent work and transformed me, I am now able to view my mother through different eyes and have come to the realization that she is, in fact, a wonderful person and I now believe that, in her own way, that she does appreciate me and love me. It is, however, unfortunate that my mother still does not know how to give or reciprocate love and affection. After years of formal education and lived experiences, I realize that it is not possible for anyone to demonstrate and give love when that person does not understand the many characteristics of love and don't actually know how to express genuine love to another person. Every child, every man and every woman must be educated on the many aspects of love and ways in which they can demonstrate that love.

We are never too young or too old to learn new things. All we really require is a willing heart. I felt a deep sense of loss and emptiness when my mother rejected me; however, since then, I have come to the understanding that my mother herself is living with the hurt of rejection. She treated me then according to her own negative experiences and rejection, which was all a part of her own upbringing. It is apparent to me that she suffered and is still suffering from the hurt and pains of rejection.

When two victims of hurt, abuse and rejection connect, the only thing that they can contribute to each other is pain and resentment. These victims must seek help and deliverance. I am happy to report that I am now entirely free from my mother's rejection, which was accomplished through the love of Christ through his Holy Spirit that dwells within me. I am so grateful to God that my mother was willing to overcome her struggles and birth me into this world.

# REFUSE TO SINK INTO THE FEAR OF REJECTION

In *"Mathew 14:30-31*(KJV),** Peter steps out of the boat with confidence, but as he walked towards Jesus, he felt a gusty wind and became fearful. He started to doubt his Christ-given abilities and potentials and began to sink. Realizing his dilemma, he cried out to God for help. Jesus immediately stretched forth his hand, caught him and said: *"O thou of little faith, wherefore didst thou doubt?"*

Why do you doubt that you are beautiful and wonderfully

made? Why do you question your ability to rise above low self-esteem and all the hurt of your past? What is it that you are focusing on that is causing you to live in fear and is influencing your mind to operate in doubt, concerning your God-given abilities to be an extraordinary person? Know this, without a doubt; you're fully equipped with the potentials to overcome every obstacle in your path through unquenchable faith in Christ Jesus.

Don't allow what you are afraid of to cause you to sink into the depression of rejection, low self-esteem and hopelessness. If you feel yourself falling or failing in any area of your life, then you know that it is time for you to cry out to Jesus for help, so that He can reach out and hold you up unto himself.

Do not allow anything or anyone to pull or push you into destruction. Do not let the devil steal what is rightfully yours.

You are alive because you are a part of God's plan, so do not question your value or worth. You are God's favoured selection, so do not allow the works of the enemy to keep you stuck in any form of rejection. You are sufficient with God's given abilities to be an extraordinary person; you are fully equipped with the potentials to overcome everything that purposed to hold you down.

Recognize that Jesus purpose for you to be on top of your impossibilities. So sink no further into lack of love for yourself, mistrust, fear and resentment, doubt, depression, pain, unforgiveness, anger and low self-esteem and rejection. That is the devil's plan for you, not God's purpose for you.

Even though you might now feel like all hope for your success is loss, it's not too late for you still have time for a chance of victory. You might not feel like it, but God has chosen you to be happy, so rise, put on courage, and take back what the devil stole from you. Claim love, happiness, joy, peace, contentment and high self-esteem in Jesus Mighty Name. King David says this in ***Psalms 62:6 (KJV): "He only is my rock and my salvation: he is my defence; I shall not be moved."***

Like King David allow Christ to be your Solid Foundation, surrender all to Him, and accept Him as your Deliverer. Let Him be your defence against rejection and low self-esteem.

# SIBLINGS REJECTION

I believe that sibling rejection usually occurs where resentment and covetousness exists. In Joseph's case, the first reason why he was resented is because of the evil report that he gave to his father Jacob about his brother.

The second was due to the fact that Jacob, seems to love him more than his brothers and demonstrated that favouritism by making him a special robe of many colours. And the third reason was based on his divine ability to dream and interpret visions. Are you a victim of sibling rejection? Are you under the perception that your parents favoured your siblings above you? As a result, you felt that you were shown less love? Unfortunately, since the beginning of time, some parents have engaged in favouritism with their children. This practice has initiated sibling rivalry, and many have taken that harmful behaviour straight into adulthood.

There are siblings, who have not spoken to each other in years, due to the damaging factors that stem from favouritism and rivalry. At age seventeen Joseph came under attack by his brothers who plotted and schemed to get rid of him.

The brothers abducted him, with the intent to kill him. They stripped him of his robe of fine colours that their father had given to him and threw him into a pit to await death.

Joseph's brother Judah decided that it would not be profitable to kill Joseph, so it was decided that they would sell him instead.

He was then taken from the pit and sold for twenty pieces of silver to traders that were related to him. But they did not acknowledge Joseph to be of much worth to them if they kept him, so they sold him into Egypt to Potiphar, a captain of Pharaoh's guards. *Gen 37:1-28, 39:1 (KJV)*

Potiphar liked Joseph and realized that he had become very successful after he brought Joseph into his home. So, he promoted Joseph and gave him the position to manage his household and all his businesses. The only person that Joseph did not have authority over was Potiphar's wife.

Potiphar's wife developed a sexual appetite for younger flesh and lusted for Joseph. She requested he engaged in sexual relations with her. But he declined her passion, by telling her that his master has set him over everything except her, and furthermore, how could he go against him in such manner, and sin against God. **But her feelings for him was already burning hot, so she tried to hold him and forced herself on him**. He ran out of the house, leaving her with his shirt in her hands. Joseph's rejection of her sexual desire for him caused her to become extremely annoyed.

She was hurt and purposed that if she cannot have Joseph; then the dungeon will. And when her husband got home, she told him that Joseph sexually molested her, and she presented his shirt as proof. Such evidence angered Potiphar to dismissed Joseph for all his liability and imprisoned him. (*Gen 39:2-20 KJV*).

# GOD'S ESTABLISHMENT OF YOU AFTER MAN REJECTS YOU

Just when Joseph thought that everything was happening for him, it vanished. But the Lord was with Joseph as his help. I realized that though rejection is depressing and makes one's life miserable, it can also work out to be one of the best afflictions ever. Based on how you will handle your mindset in battle. Why did I say that? Think well about this: Joseph was very talented, but if his brothers did not reject him, he would've not been able to become the ruler that he was born to be.

Sometimes it takes people's rejection and false testimony of you to bring you into your purpose. In Joseph's case, it was proven to be true. Joseph was born not to be a ruler over Potiphar household and his substances but over the whole house of Egypt, including Potiphar and his wife. He was purposed to be the second ruler over Egypt, but if he had remained as Potiphar's assistant then the gift in him that God will to make room for him, to place him in the presence of Pharaoh, would have become unproductive to him. *Prov 18:16 KJV* says, *"A man's gift maketh room for him and bringeth him before great men."*

In *Gen 41:1-46 (KJV)* the showcasing of his potential and abilities concerning dreams, and the interpretations of them, were not needed in Potiphar's house but in the dungeon. Yes! A dungeon is the last place that anyone would want to be.

So, Potiphar's wife's rejection of Joseph's integrity and her lies about him were indeed the perfect opportunities that Joseph needed, even though he couldn't understand it at the time. God used Joseph's gifts to facilitate his rise from the dungeon, where at age thirty, he stood in the presence of Pharaoh, ruler of Egypt, to interpret dreams. It was God who ultimately made Joseph rise like a phoenix, into the position of ruler of Egypt.

Let Joseph's story motivate and empower you, and help you to rise out of rejection, low self-esteem, failure, unforgiveness, discouragement, depression, anger, or whatever demonic influences you are currently battling within your life. Know that God can do all things, primarily he can deliver you out of any dungeon. *"Now to him who is able to do exceedingly abundantly above all that we ask or think, according to the power that works in us, to Him be glory in the church by Christ Jesus to all generations, forever and ever. Amen!" Eph 3:20 (NKJV).*

**The Lord can help you beyond your requests and thoughts. What is difficult for you is but a light thing for Him**. Allow Him to keep you from falling into the hurt of rejection and low self-esteem unworthy feelings. Let Christ keep you from falling into bitterness, anger, resentment, fear and unbelief. Joseph looked unto Him, and he abundantly helped him. With the Lord's help, he was able to use rejection as a pathway to achieve great success. Look unto the Lord Jesus and take authority over every rejection influence, for, with his strength, you cannot and will not fail.

# USE REJECTION TO UNLOCK\
## YOUR PURPOSE

Joseph's rejections were the keys to unlock the purpose for which he was born. Don't allow the lies, humiliation, shame, pain and resentment of rejection to imprison you. Use your experiences of rejection to bring out your hidden treasures. Let those experiences open the doors that the enemy has closed and explore your abilities.

Refuse to allow rejection to terminate your gifts and abilities. Don't permit the hurt of rejection to bind you and keep you in unforgiveness captivity. Joseph was willing to forgive his siblings because he understood the reason for his refusal. He realizes that it was not about his brothers, because their rejection of him was Godly authorized. It was all a part of God's plan to turn what they meant for evil against him into good for his father's household. *Gen 45:1-8.*

Likewise, God has already turned your refusal into your favour, so don't make resentment, and hurt cause you to decline your season to reap the benefits of living a happy life. Don't give rejection the upper hand in your life. If you do that, then you will be jeopardizing your mindset. Knowing that the spirit of refusal purpose is to make sure that you live and fail, to accomplish the standard of life that God design for you to enjoy. Joseph was determined not to be a prisoner of any form of rejection hurt. I also encourage you to do the same.

Suggested readings: *Genesis chapters 37, 39 & 47 (KJV).*

## DEFEATING THE THREE MAIN GUARDS OF REJECTION

The three main guards of refusal are lack of love, unwillingness to forgive and resentment. To overcome rejection, you must first defeat its guards with the two most potent weapons, the love of Christ and his forgiveness.

Sometimes the person whom you resent is also the person who God has purposed to contribute to the building up of your life in general. But you block whatsoever help that God will to come to you from whomever, because of the hurts others have caused you to experience. Don't allow unforgiveness to hold you in the confinement of vindictiveness. **Leave all vengeance to God and be free from the pain of rejection.**

The goal of rejection is intended to rob you from living a productive and joyful life. **Refuse to surrender your emotions to pride and do not unauthorize any blessings that are approved by God.** For many people, it has been a challenging task to forgive, and with an open-arm, accept anyone who has offended and rejected them.

However, forgiveness is not an option. It is a direct command from God. *"For if ye forgive men their trespasses, your heavenly Father will also forgive you: but if ye forgive not men their trespasses, neither will your Father forgive your* trespasses" (*Matthew 6:14-15 KJV*). Therefore, in obedience to God's directive, it is mandatory that you forgive those who have and still do initiate and perpetuate abuse and torment in your life. **Forgiveness is paramount in breaking the yoke of**

**rejection. It is the pathway that is mandatory to provide you with the much-needed peace of mind towards those who attack you**. Forgiveness will also separate and remove the sourness of resentment from your emotions and stimulate sweetness in your mindset.

It is noted in the book of Acts chapter 9 that, professed followers of the Lord Jesus Christ rejected the Apostle Paul and his ministry because he had imposed torment upon them. Paul opposed salvation by grace through faith in the Lord Jesus Christ. He was significantly influenced by the teaching of the Law of Moses, which he upheld in self-righteousness.

Paul was enthusiastic with the desire to gain legal power to arrest and bound anyone who proposed to be a follower of Christ. In his endeavours to persecute those who fail to remain loyal to the Law of Moses, he encounters a Christ intervention, which blinded him for three days and transformed him from Saul the Pharisee to Paul the Apostle.

Paul went from being a student of Moses to become Jesus' pupil. He went from desiring to kill Jews to being passion-filled for them to be saved. Paul was approved and appointed by Christ to be His chosen vessel to carry the gospel unto the Gentiles, rulers of nations and the children of Israel. **It is important to note that although the Lord Jesus Christ may come into your heart, reform you to undertake a position of authority and influence, it doesn't mean that everyone in your past whom you offended, will welcome you into their lives, or treat you as a friend.** While some individuals may ultimately see, comprehend and acknowledge your positive transformation and forgive you for whatever past pain you had inflicted on them before your acceptance of the Lord

Jesus Christ into your life, others may not be as willing to believe or forgive. Even when God instructs people who knew of your horrible past deeds to assist you, it may be difficult for them to do so. While people's rejection of you will be brutal and discouraging, you will have to keep your eyes on Christ. Embrace his love and embed your faith and hope in him. *Acts 9:13* says, *"Then Ananias answered, Lord, I have heard by many of this man, how much evil he hath done to thy saints at Jerusalem." (KJV).*

It is the nature of the *Adamic self* to struggle to see beyond the violations that someone has committed. Ananias, the high priest, was willing to deny himself to see Paul in the manner in which God saw him, and was then able to bless him accordingly. However, Even though Ananias laid hands on Paul, healed him entirely from his three days of blindness, baptized him as a disciple of Jesus Christ, the majority of believers still did not care about Paul's conversion and rejected him and his ministry. *Acts 9:21* (KJV) states, *"But all that heard him were amazed, and said; Is not this he that destroyed them which called on this name in Jerusalem, and came hither for that intent, that he might bring them bound unto the chief priests?"* Although in *verse 24* of the same chapter, you will read that Paul delivered powerful sermons concerning Jesus Christ, the people were still determined to kill him. **Many of the people who professed then, to be followers of Christ would have rather seen Paul dead than to forgive him**. Yet, in him, were their blessings. Every information and revelation that they needed to improve their mindset into the righteousness of God in Christ was deposit into the Apostle Paul. It was there for them to withdraw and become rich in the grace of God's teaching through faith. But many died in self-righteousness just because they chose not to forgive him of rejecting them in his past.

I genuinely admire the Apostle Paul enthusiasm. It's not simple to stand in the presence of an audience of people who detest and refuse you along with your good intentions towards them. But Paul's focus was not centred on the peoples' rejection of him. He was determined never to allow anyone or anything to detour him from fulfilling his God's given abilities and performances.

In like manner, terminate from your mindset every negative saying and disapproval of you. **Some folks will never stop watching the series of your past, neither will they cease from discussing your past characters. You need to understand that you can't stop them. But you can prevent YOU from becoming a subject of their reduction calculation of your Gods' purposed talent and mandate for your life.**

Some people will refuse you, with the mindset that you will become subjected and tormented by their rejection of you. They are confident that you will not survive to be of anything good, or even achieve a satisfying life. You must reject such influence, and believe; that you can, and will be, what God will.

# ACCEPTING THE UNDERSTANDING OF REJECTION

Please bear in mind that I am not promoting any reason to justify rejection, and I am not saying that you should accept rejection, but I do strongly recommend that you comprehend it. Why should you? **Because the understanding of the**

**dismissal will not cause you to forget, but it will help you to reverse hatred through love and help to heal you from the hurts that denial imposed upon you.** It will also strengthen you to forgive anyone who rejects you.

Take a moment to reflect on Joseph's life and his experience with rejection. Remember that he was only seventeen years old when he was rejected by his brothers, and sold for twenty pieces of silver. The first buyer resold him to Potiphar, who loved Joseph as a trusted friend and later came to love him as a son. Potiphar treated Joseph with incredible kindness and respect for about eleven years. However, when his wife framed Joseph, he turned his incredible generosity into full wrath. In the book of Genesis Joseph dealt with three significant rejections, which significantly impacted his life, but what I admire most about him, is that he never allowed the pains of disappointments and rejection to discourage, depress, devalue or control his mindset. He guarded his emotions and conducted himself with high esteem, grace and honour, knowing without a doubt that God would deliver him from every attack or persecution that he encountered in his life.

While the hurts of rejection were legitimate, fierce and brutal, Joseph refused to allow rejection to manipulate and control his desire to succeed. **Joseph's attitude reminds me of the sunlight, and the hurt and rejection he experienced are like the cloud. At times the clouds may get in the way of the sunshine, but the sun never ceases to shine. Start seeing yourself like that unstoppable sunshine!**

# REFUSE TO DIE IN SELF-REJECTION

Some people might say that they would rather die than have to experience all of the rejections and pains that Joseph encountered. We can only speculate that when Joseph was in the dungeon, there may have been times when depression attacked his mind and could have caused him to feel defeated. However, when the cloud of rejection sought to cover his mind, he just kept shining like the sun.

**Just like Joseph, you don't have to live in the devastation and devaluation of rejection; similar to the sun, God intends for you to shine even in the coldest and darkest days.** Through God's grace, you can break through any cloud of rejection that comes into your mind to prevent you from shining and enjoying his love, peace and happiness. *"For I know the thoughts that I think toward you, saith the Lord, thoughts of peace, and not of evil, to give you* an expected end."* Jeremiah 29:11 (KJV).

# FRIENDS' REJECTION

Jesus was rejected by the best of his friends, but He did not allow the refusal of his friends to conquer his emotions. His heart and mind were filled with love and forgiveness towards everyone, giving them a choice to consider Him. A kiss of rejection and betrayal is what Judas gave in return for Jesus' love after he pocketed thirty pieces of silver to lie on Christ. Even though Jesus knew in advance that Judas would betray him, He still embraced and interacted with Judas in love and considered him a friend. *Matthew 26:15 & 47-50 (KJV)*. **I don't know who may have rejected and betrayed you and handed you over to die. Do not allow other people's rejection of you to dominate your emotions. An emotion that is consists of sad feelings, resentment, unforgiveness, hatred, anger and bitterness, will be all negative and destructive. As long as you continue to invest in those types of feelings towards the people who have rejected you, then you'll always remain as a prisoner of rejection.**

In order to make rejection completely powerless, you need to be like Jesus Christ, embracing love and forgiveness and generate them towards everyone who rejects you. Lies, betrayal and denial seem to work together in complete harmony to produce destruction. This ultimately is the devil's plan for our lives. After Judas had betrayed Jesus, he was left with a heavy burden on his heart due to the wicked act that he had undertaken against Christ.

He tried to reverse his betrayal by seeking to speak with the chief priest and elders to counter his lies, speak the truth and return the thirty pieces of silver, but they refused to listen and rejected his attempt. Their rejection, compounded with low self-esteem, was able to affect Judas's emotions. He saw himself as useless and worthless. The burden of the lies that he had told on Jesus and his inability to correct the situation, propelled Judas into a state of depression and defeat. Judas could not live with the burden of what he had done and took his life by hanging on a tree. *Matthew 27:1-5 (KJV)*.

Unfortunately, Judas was not the only one to betray Christ. Another person who Jesus called a friend was Peter, who on three occasions, also rejected and denied knowing Christ.

*John 18:15-27 (KJV)*. Jesus declined the hurt and fear of rejection and demonstrated love and forgiveness towards Peter. *John 21:15-17 (KJV)*. Jesus understood well that Peter's denial of him was the devil's plan to destroy His mandate for Peter's life. It was also to get Peter to abort his abilities (Luke 22:31-34). But Peter was able to overcome the devil's rejection scheme because he loves and believes in Jesus and his words.

You can break every shackle of rejection, hurt, anger, unforgiveness, fear, low self-esteem and depression from your emotions and your entire life by completely loving Jesus, through obedience to his words. You might feel like you can't climb out from the deep hole where rejection has taken you, but you can, and will if you embrace love and forgiveness. When you accept that you deserve to live in love and be determined in your mind to achieve it no matter what comes in your way, then you shall have victory over rejection and all its attachments.

# REJECTION AFTER RAPE

In *2 Samuel 13:1-19*, you will find a disturbing rape incident that was carried out by Amnon, King David's son with his half-sister Tamar. He was utterly obsessed with her and often fell into angry and a depressive state because of his intense feelings for her. Amnon wanted to get Tamar's attention but was clueless in matters of how to get her to fulfil his passion. Jonadab, Amnon's first cousin and close friend, was fed-up with Amnon's self-pity and was determined to know why his cousin appeared to be in a grumpy mood.

When Jonadab questioned him, Amnon confided in him

and revealed his intimate feelings for his sister. Jonadab, being a very deceitful and conniving person, encouraged Amnon to go in his bed and pretend to be sick. He advised Amnon when his father King David came to visit him, he should request to have Tamar bake for him, which would provide him with the opportunity that he needed. King David approved Amnon's request and sent Tamar to fulfill the duties. Tamar dutifully baked the cakes of his choice. When she completed the task and presented it to him in the company of his guards, he did not take it from her.

He gave the order for all his guards to depart and instructed that his sister present the cakes to him in his bedchamber. Amnon then took advantage of his sister who tried to get him to reconsider what he was doing by telling him, that his actions would not be permittable in Israel, but he ignored her and refused to listen.

Tamar put up fierce resistance, but he was stronger than her and proceeded to rape her. After violating her, he hated her more than the lustful feelings he had for her because he expected that she would have been a willing participant in his disgusting plot. He demanded that she leave his quarters, but she pleaded with him not to reject her in such a cold and demeaning manner because it was a rejection worse than the rape. *2 Samuel 13:16* says, *"And she said unto him, there is no cause: this evil in sending me away is greater than the other that thou didst unto me. But he would not harken unto her."* (KJV).

Amnon did not want to hear anything that she had to say, so he called his guard to throw her out and bolt the door behind her. Presently in the world, many women and men are now suffering from the consequences of the violation and rejection of rape. This type of assault can have permanent severe effects on us. Without deliverance, counselling and healing, many victims have found themselves engaging in appalling and indecent sexual behaviours. Prostitution and same-sex relationships are where many people have testified that their broken lives have taken them after they were raped, devalued and rejected. In my opinion, these types of criminal, abusive and demoralizing experiences produce some of the highest levels of low self-esteem. It has also been associated with many issues that couples have experienced. Rape has been the source of many conflicts in relationships, and sadly, in some cases, has led to divorce.

Pray this prayer. *"Heavenly Father thou God who sits in the highest realm. I accept your redemption for my life and deny myself unto thee. Let your dominion now come in this earthly vessel as it is in Heaven. By your authority command the powers that are depressing my mindset to go from me. Take full control of my emotions, by your dominion, let every thought and imaginations that seek to exalt themselves against my knowledge of you, to be cast down in captivity in obedience to you. Let your will be done in this earthily vessel as it is in Heaven. I accept your forgiveness and also forgive those who hurt me. In your Mighty Name, I renounce the powers of my flesh and surrender all of my feelings to your Reign. By faith in you, I now decline my own will. I pray that only your proposed will be done in my life. I denounce the intent of my past. Through your love, grace and mercy, I renounce rejection partnership, and all low self-esteem degrading feelings. I renounce all unrighteousness, I renounce condemnation, I renounce generation curses, I renounce sexual curses, I renounce unforgiveness*

*curses, witchcraft curses, I renounce finical curses, I complete-*
*ly renounce every curse upon my life in the name of Jesus, and*
*I accept your blessings for my life in Christ Jesus, my lord. By*
*the power of your Holy Spirit command the capabilities of my*
*past, to be broken off my mindset.*

*Through your name of Jesus Christ, I believe that I am free*
*entirely from the anxiety of rape, rejection hurt, and the luck of*
*acceptance of myself. Like a hen cover her chickens let your re-*
*demption blood cover my emotions, from every effects and resi-*
*due of my past afflictions. Help me daily to acknowledge you in*
*all of my doing, so that, your word can guide my feelings into*
*productive motivations. I declare that you are my everlasting*
*Father, you alone are the wonderful counsellor of my mindset*
*and ruler of my contentment. Thank you for making condemna-*
*tion powerless in my life. I give you thanks for being there for*
*me, even when I thought that you did not care about me. To you*
*be all the glory, honour and praises, now and forever in Jesus*
*Name, I pray amen."*

## REJECTION IN MARRIAGES WHERE RAPE HAS OCCURRED

There is an unlawful sexual bonding that is activated when someone experiences rape. Please do not use what I am going to explain in the next few paragraphs, to blame yourself for the reprehensible act that was committed against you.

I hope that this information will help to heal you and cause you to move on with your life. When your right to say no, was violated, by the force of the rapist, you were willing to maintain your no, by putting up resistance, which included excess struggling. For instance, now you are a married woman, and you tell your husband about the rape, but he has no understanding of the symptoms of such a violation.

He is getting frustrated a lot, and very disappointed and discouraged because he is wondering why when he wants to hold you and kiss you, in most of the attempt you keep pushing him off. He always has to struggle with you whenever he desires to engage in intimacy with you.

He is frustrated as to why you would be enjoying his advances, and then all of a sudden you want him to stop and abort. He has no understanding that you are behaving in such a manner because of your violent first sexual encounter. He is not aware that sometimes his approach and his touch, and the way he kisses, and the way he makes love with you, is causing you to have a difficult time trying to differentiate. You are experiencing an emotional conflict, and it is causing your mindset to fluctuate.

So, if you decline to get the necessary help to recover from rape rejection pain, then such refusal will destroy your relationship because the pain of the rape released mistrust in you towards men. Mentally you are angry with man, but physically you purpose to have one. You're not willing to give in, and let him see how loving you can be because of your insecurity.

In the case where it is the husband that was rape, the wife would observe similar behaviour. Rape is divided into different categories such as incestual, which means that the perpetrator committing the offence is a blood relation such as father, brother, uncle, cousin or other close family members.

Rape is committed by spouses, casual intimate partners,

individuals viewed as friends or by strangers. Regardless of the category, rape produces trauma, pain, hurt, insecurity, brokenness, rejection and low self-esteem. In some cases, people are raped repeatedly by the same offender, and unfortunately, this can occur over several years, without being detected or disclosed. Some people have been able to get deliverance from the traumatic experience of rape and the adverse side-effects, after receiving salvation in Christ.

Some victims of rape do share their experiences with their spouses, while others chose to remain silent on the matter. It is my opinion that sharing your traumatic experience with your spouse is crucial to the success of your marriage. For any couple to be happy and live in unity, trust has to be established. Trust must be a part of the foundation of every marriage, along with love, respect, honesty and patience. Intimacy is a tremendous characteristic of any marriage, so failure to share your painful experience with your spouse will inevitably affect your relationship and marriage.

Rejection will ultimately play a significant role in that relationship if you don't let your spouse know what had occurred earlier in your life. There is no guarantee that after making your spouse aware that you were raped, that your spouse would truly comprehend the issues that you may be experiencing in the intimate aspect of your relationship. This is precisely why there cannot be secrets in a marriage.

Professional counselling and therapy must be sought to allow for the couple to get the necessary support that they require. Believers should not seek counsel outside of the church because the strategic approach of addressing issues may not be in standing with the word of God. *Psalms 1:1(KJV) states,*

*"Blessed is the man that walketh not in the counsel of the wicked, nor standeth in the way of sinners, nor sitteth in the seat of the scornful."*

Many victims of rape are still struggling within, but are determined to overcome their trauma. Years later, others are still living in brokenness and feel confined by the horrible abusive experience. Depression and low self-esteem cause those people to feel like they don't have any self-worth. Some people think that they are "damaged" and will never be able to get married or have a normal life. **Those negative beliefs are fuelled by rejection and low self-esteem.**

**I encourage you to stop seeing yourself as the victim of any form of bondage, whether rape, anger, regret, unforgiveness, pains, hurt, brokenness and insecurity. The truth is, you are more than a "conqueror and overcomer," even though you might not even realize it.**

Start believing that you are fearful and wonderfully made because you are! Believe that you are worthy of happiness because you are worthy! Rise and give God all the honour, praise, glory and thanks for life. Forgive those that have raped, offended and rejected you throughout your life. Show your spouse love, trust, respect, honour and patience.

Remember, do not keep secrets from each other, especially secrets that can damage your relationship and end your marriage. **I speak strength into your life to break the chains of weakness, courage to break the fetters of confusion and joy to break the bands of unhappiness in your life, in the Mighty Name of Jesus Christ!**

Declare in the Name of Jesus that the trauma of rape shall not intensify in your down siting, in your uprising, going out or coming in. You are not a subject to the hurt of rape. Deny the anxiety effects thereof and embrace a quality mindset in your relationship.

You are unique, unusual and is entirely worthy of love, to love and be loved. You are not a secondary you belong in first place. Also, you are not a leftover; you are the served portion. You might feel like a failure and already convinced yourself that you are nothing. But that's a deception, stop believing it to be true.

You're not a hopeless person, your dreams are not dead. Be determined in your feelings to rise from the pit of scorn. Accept the grace of God, and be confident of his love for you. Also, start to appreciate you and love you as a person who deserve to be treated exceptionally.

Don't allow the hurt and insecurity of your past to influence you into believing that you are a captive of rejection or any low self-esteem devaluation of yourself.

# THE DEVIL'S DESIRE IS FOR YOU TO REJECT YOURSELF

It is the devil's desire for you to reject yourself and be disqualified by others. It is much easier to overcome the rejection of others than personal rejection. Those who suffer from two-fold rejection will experience more rejection afflictions as opposed to those with a single-fold.

Rejection will create feelings of confusion in your life to prevent you from accepting your worth. These feelings will also promote and influence doubt in your mindset and cause you to second guess your abilities. Rejection will blindfold you so that you will not be able to recognize or comprehend the appreciation of yourself. It's the devil's intention for you to view yourself through the eyes of judgemental negative people. So, practice avoiding the turmoil associated with rejection. Regardless of any setbacks that you may experience in your life, know that God's evaluation of you is unchangeable. He loves you, and you must, in turn, love yourself.

# THE CAUSES OF SELF-REJECTION

Silent rejection is the activator of personal or self-rejection. Silent rejection is one of the most self-destructive influences against the conception of self-worth. It is the womb in which self-refusal is conceived. It is also is the battlefield where low self-esteem dominates you and become superior in your emotions.

In the book of Job chapter 2:11-12, Job's friends stood silently before him for seven days and nights because they recognized that he has suffered significant loss and was in a place of deep darkness and depression. Job did not understand the reason for their silence, and he felt intimidated, insulted and rejected by them. Job allowed the fear of rejection to access his mindset and low self-esteem. Such authorization compels him to explore and embrace the ruin energy effects of rejection.

Job was an honourable man who loved and respected God. He was a man of high esteem and a very successful businessman. But when Job believed that his three friends had rejected him, he felt an overwhelming amount of hurt and fell into a deep depression. Those unproductive feelings caused Job to view himself as useless, worthless and loveless.

He cursed his conception, his present and future. However, in spite of the sufferings and turmoil that Job experienced, he chose to look unto God for help, and it was with that level of faith, he was able to overcome self-rejection, his friend's rejection and low self-esteem. Although God's intervention did not occur overnight, Job's complete belief in God was so firm, that it provided him with the courage to trust and wait until God answered his prayers. At the end of his bitter trials, he had total deliverance from the possession of self- rejection, low self-esteem, depression and rejection from his friends. Ultimately, Job was blessed with a double for his trouble. (Suggest reading Job chapter 42).

Job's experience can happen to anyone. Maybe you have already had a similar experience or currently going through one as you are reading this book. Do not become discouraged due to the intensity of the problem that you are facing. Job chose to go through his challenging season alone, waiting on God. God is, in fact, the answer to every problem.

You are more than a conqueror; you were born as an overcomer, created in God's image and likeness. You are more than a conqueror you were born as an extraordinary achiever, not a dysfunctional person, but a capable being, not impotent, but strong and sturdy, not sorrowful, but joyful, inspirational and courageous. In *Matthew 19:26 (NKJV)*, **Jesus** said, *"With men, this is impossible, but with God all things are possible."*

# ALWAYS DECLINE THE MENTAL VOICE OF SELF-REJECTION

To reject yourself is to abort God's mandate and purpose for your life, and by doing so, you will have willingly surrendered your gifts, talents and abilities to the devil. Don't give in to self-rejection or any other form of rejection. Refuse to allow low self-esteem and depression to enslave your mindset with feelings that fuel you to showcase dysfunctional behaviours. It is essential that you understand that by telling yourself, that you are the fault when you're not the reason at all, the effects of self-rejection and low self- esteem can become registered in your emotions. This is done through such mental communication. It can also happen through verbal communication. This is when you are listening to others opinion and confirming their negative information into your mind. It is therefore crucial that you do not allow your negative thoughts and the negative words uttered by other people, to ruin your positive mindset and dictate your life.

Rejection is very dangerous and does, unfortunately, have the power to cause life-long catastrophic suffering and damage to the human mind and the physical body. Do not allow other people's exclusion and rejection of you, to impact and devastate you. Never let refusal make you question if you are "good enough" to fit in or to be a part of any group. Whether it be work, social or otherwise.

If there are people who will not communicate or engage with you, do not allow that to frustrate or put you into a state of depression. The way you were conceived, where you were born and who your parents are should not dictate who you are.

It is my firm belief that no one was born to live in depression, low self-esteem, fear and rejection.

Sometimes it might feel like you're not achieving your goals or progressing in life, but you already have the victory. All you have to do is maintain confidence in God, and the turbulence of rejection shall not prevent your flight of happiness. Let go and let God pilot your emotions, and with absolute courage, nothing and no one will be able to stop you from receiving God's peace and obtaining high self-worth.

# USE THE LADDER OF REJECTION TO YOUR ADVANTAGE

The function of a ladder is to assist people in accessing levels that would generally be beyond their average reach. The ladder of rejection is designed by the devil to take you down from high esteem into low self-esteem. If you allow a situation to cause you to choose the ladder down into the fears of rejection or low self-esteem, upon arrival, you will need to decide whether to climb out of it or allow yourself to become bound by it.

The choice is yours to determine if you would like to stay in depression, hurt and fear. If you decide not to climb up, then you will have chosen to maintain rejection, along with the behaviours and emotions associated with it, such as depression, fear, hurt, loneliness, mistrust, low-self-esteem and brokenness. Should you decide to climb up, you will be required to make the sacrifice to step above all of the strongholds of your rejection.

# DON'T ALLOW YOUR EMOTIONS TO SHOWCASE REJECTION

If you don't have a reasonable understanding of who you are and what your purpose is in life, then other people's evaluation of you can cause you to doubt your capabilities. Do not allow inferiority, insecurity, rejection and low self- esteem to create turmoil in your emotions and dictate who you are.

I encourage you to draw closer to God and develop a real relationship with him. Find out what his purpose is for your life because he created you in his image and likeness. *"So God created man in his own image, in the image of God created he him; male and female created he them." Genesis 1:27 (KJV).* As I shared with you earlier in this book, you are not a product of rejection and do not allow anyone to tell you differently.

Regardless of the odds that are working against you, stand your ground to overcome adversities. Place your full trust in God; he will always make a way when one does not seem possible. Choose to love yourself as a wonderfully made person. *Psalms 139:14* states, *"I will praise thee; for I am fearfully and wonderfully made: marvellous are thy works; and that my soul knoweth right well." (KJV).*

If you believe that you are a failure, I am here to tell you that you are not. The issues that you may have faced or is still experiencing are not bigger than you and certainly not bigger than God. Do not allow hopelessness to intimidate or overpower you. The experiences of rejection that you have encountered do not determine your end result. There will be mountains and valleys in your life's path, but you must be committed to stay on course as God has intended. Don't enable the hurts and devaluation of rejection, insecurity and low self-esteem, to cause you to be "**broken**". You deserve to be happy, so don't allow anyone or anything to rob you of that right.

## REJECTION DEPLETES TRUST

A man who suffered neglect and rejection from his mother and did not get deliverance, will not be able to treat the woman in his life with the love, honour and respect that is required. That man who has not received deliverance will harbour hate, resentment, pain, unforgiveness, insecurity and more. Such harbouring is a direct result of the fear of neglect and rejection that he suffered as a child growing up.

Likewise, a woman who suffered from her father's neglect and rejection will find it difficult to trust, submit and honour the man in her life. It is essential to add that many people grew up with both biological parents residing in the same home, and although these adults were physically present, they were emotionally and spiritually absent from their children's lives. Some people will sadly share that the only type of interaction that they had with one or both parents, would be when they were on the receiving end of insults or physical abuse.

It is excruciating for many men and women to admit that they were victims of rape by the hands of their fathers, brothers and other male relatives. In the last few years both women and men have slowly begun to speak out against the violence and intrusion that they encountered not just with relatives or friends, but with respected members of the community such as priests, pastors, coaches and teachers, to only name a few. Those were converted positions of trust, but clearly, these immoral men and women breached when they chose to violate and compromise their positions of authority. Many believers, both men and women have gone through life facing one critical challenge after another, rejection after rejection and have failed to recognize the unresolved issues, which has caused them to miss out on the mountain-top-life that our Heavenly Father intended us to have.

All issues connected with neglect, rejection, abuse, anger, unforgiveness, distrust and low self-esteem are designed by the enemy to destroy us. In *John 10:10-11,* Jesus said: *"The thief cometh not, but to kill, steal and destroy: I come that they might have life, and they might have it more abundantly." I am the good shepherd: the good shepherd giveth his life for the sheep" (KJV).*

Jesus clearly states that in spite of the attacks of the enemy, in spite of the pains *and* torment that you have faced and may still be facing, that you can have faith and trust in him because he will give his life for you. As we all know today, Jesus Christ did sacrifice his life for us. I do not know of one living human here on earth who would do that for me.

Do you know of such a man who would sacrifice his life for you? I encourage you to place all of your trust in our Precious Lord and Saviour, for he is the only one who can deliver you from your challenges. He did it for me, and he can certainly do it for you. Just trust him!

# DO NOT INVEST YOUR MINDSET IN REJECTION

Rejection in totality is really, ruin energy, joint earning contract and turmoil in one's nature. Investing in self-rejection or the rejection of others is unproductive and ineffective for your daily life. So don't invest your mindset in the rotten energy of refusal and the feelings of deprecation.

The result will be nothing but turmoil, which is a state of great disturbance, confusion or uncertainty. Refuse to settle in the mindset of ruin energy, which will continually keep you in confused states of unproductive behaviours, unhappiness and self-resentment.

# NEVER BE DECEIVED BY REJECTION

Once God abides within you; rejection will not be able to penetrate your mind, body or soul. Keep your eyes upon God and keep believing in Him regardless of the challenges that you may have to face. Only the Lord Jehovah God alone can deliver you from all problems. *Psalms 34:19 (KJV)* states, "**Many** *are the afflictions of the righteous: but the Lord delivereth him out of them all.*"

*Love and appreciate yourself and dismiss all reports of rejection. Refuse to allow other people's negative, unjust and hurtful opinions to upset, frustrate and put you into any depressive state. It's God's opinion that truly counts, and with his help, you are going to be happy, successful and unstoppable!*

# DON'T SUBJECT YOUR YOUTHFULNESS TO REJECTION

In *1 Timothy 4:12,* the apostle Paul encouraged and taught his spiritual son, Timothy, in the true teachings of Christ. He told him not to allow anyone to despise his youth due to the way he was conceived. People viewed Timothy as an undervalued person. Why did others reject Timothy? *Acts 16:1-3* stated that Timothy's mother was a Jewish woman who believed in the Lord Jesus. Timothy was also a disciple of Jesus, but his father was Greek. As a result, the Jews of Lystra and Iconium did not consider Timothy a person of much significance, because he was the son of a Greek man. It was reported among the believing Jews that he was of mixed-race parentage.

Do not allow "religious people" who may know things about your past life before you came to Christ, to reject your salvation in Christ and despise the gifts and skills that God has deposited within you. Your God-given gifts and abilities don't need any approval from humankind to function because they are already Holy Spirit authorized.

The apostle Paul loved Timothy and spent a significant amount of time, encouraging him to become bold and always to acknowledge his God-given abilities. However, Timothy continued to struggle in his ministry because he was afraid of being despised. Why was Timothy so timid? It was because he possessed low self-esteem; was spiritually weak and blind to his true identity. This mindset prevented him from what he was called to be. The Holy Spirit appointed him through the apostle

Paul as the pastor of the Ephesian church. However, even with such honour, the older believers continuously challenged him and his rank as a pastor, due to his young age.

Nevertheless, as a young pastor, he was getting very weary of proving himself to gain acceptance. He was tired of being despised, and this is what the apostle Paul, his mentor, told him as recorded in *1 Tim 4:14 (KJV)*, *"Neglect not the gift that is in thee, which was given thee by prophecy, with the laying on of the hands of the elders."* But Timothy was now at a point in life where he did not care anymore about what the Holy Spirit declared to him or even the gift that Christ delivered unto him through the elders of the church, which was deposited by their laying of hands upon him.

Even then, the apostle Paul encouraged him to continue to care for what God has called him to do and not to ignore the abilities and talents that God placed in him. The apostle Paul recognized that Timothy was not functioning at the level of the gifts and talents that he possessed. Paul also noticed that Timothy was avoiding preaching and teaching on Christ' ministry and was further distancing himself from Paul. In *2 Timothy 1:5-8*, the apostle Paul again wrote to Timothy to encourage him to overcome his fear. The apostle Paul stated in verse *5* that the faith that Timothy had was pure and sincere, a faith without hypocrisy.

Timothy's grandmother and mother also possessed the same gifts. The apostle Paul told Timothy that though he was not sure that he possessed the same faith as his grandmother and mother, he, Paul, was convinced that the same faith and teachings were in Timothy. It can be challenging when someone recognizes particular gifts and talents in you, and make you aware of them, but due to your ignorance and lack of spiritual sight, you reject the counsel and guidance.

The apostle Paul again instructs Timothy to STIR UP (refresh or keep in full flame) the gift of God in him. *In 2 Timothy 1:6 "the gift of God"* is regarded as a fire capable of dying out through neglect. Therefore, in order for Timothy's ministry to stay alive, he had to apply boldness to keep it blazing. Fear, lack of love and unstable thinking was causing the fire of the gift that God had placed in him to fade away slowly. Timothy's ministry was not blazing because he was sourcing it with the fuel of fear which God did not give to him. Timothy allowed the fear of the devil to enter and interrupt God's ministry.

**Do you see yourself in Timothy?** Are you aware of your Christ-given gifts and abilities, but afraid to rise and undertake the assignments that you are given because you do not want to face rejection? If your behaviours resemble those of Timothy, then this message is for you. God did not give you the spirit of fear. He gave you the Spirit of love, of power and a sound mind. Do not allow fear of any kind to cause you to neglect the gifts and talents that Christ has bestowed upon you. Refuse to allow the rejection of others, to cause you to bury your God-given gifts and abilities because what God started in you, He is more than able to finish. **Philippians 1:6 (KJV)** says, **"being confident of this very thing, that he which hath begun a good work in you will perform it until the day of Jesus Christ."**

# DO NOT BECOME INTIMIDATED BY THE THREAT OF REJECTION

In *1 Kings 19:1-5,* Jezebel despised and rejected Elijah, and when Elijah heard of her rejection of him, it strengthened his low self-esteem and caused him to surrender his emotions to depression and oppression. Such persuasion caused him to subject his mindset to suicidal thoughts. He accepted the spirit of fear and stopped loving himself, devaluing himself to the level of uselessness and worthlessness.

He was a mighty prophet of God but allowed himself to get weary in doing his job. Regardless of the difficulties or circumstances that you may be facing, refuse to give up and die. Do not surrender your mindset to the ruin energy of rejection. Be not afraid of any threat that rejection may seek to use in order to break your positive mindset. Those who despise you will only trump to victory if you accept their influences of intimidation and condemnation.

# YOUR DAILY LIVING BECOMES WHAT YOU ACCEPT

Acceptance of rejection is an ability binder that prevents the development of potentials and leads to living a life driven by cowardliness. It is your responsibility to guard your God-given gifts and abilities against anyone who seeks to destroy them and you. Abilities are the gifts and talents that the Holy Spirit gave you and potential is the ability to develop those gifts and talents. God created you with the maximum capabilities to undertake any tasks or endeavour that he has assigned to you.

When you live in Christ and he abides in you, your capacity is uncapped and your God-given potentials and abilities are not prisoners of fear, not covered by doubt, or sealed with discouragement, oppression or weaknesses. They are covered by eternal strength. *In Philippians 4:13(KJV),* when the apostle Paul recognized the supernatural abilities that he possessed, he said, *"I can do all things through Christ who supports me with strength."*

The fear of rejection will cause you to hide in torment, to run away from trials and to accept defeat without a fight. It will also cause you to abort your purpose and give birth to fear. The devil realizes that if he uses someone to reject you, then you will become more susceptible to hurt and confusion.

Timothy was exhausted, trying to prove his credibility and seeking to gain acceptance.

Do not get weary in attempting to gain approval from people. That is not the role that God has called you to undertake. God's approval is the only one that you must obtain. He is the one who will pour favour upon you. If you deny God and follow the directives of man, then you will be disappointed, frustrated and unhappy.

**Stop looking for people's acceptance of you. Embrace and approve yourself as an exceptional and peculiar child of God. Not everyone will bask in your accomplishments. Close friends and families will also despise you, because of their jealousy of you.**

What you accept daily in your living is entirely your choice to chose. If you receive the rotten energy of rejection, and low self-esteem reproachful feelings, then you will be burden down thereby. You are not a subject to the brokenness of rejection or the scornful feelings of low self-esteem.

See yourself to be above and not beneath, the head and not the tail, secure and not weak. You were not born into this world to be or live as scorn. Decline everything that you accept that is not making life better for you, and receive the things that Christ authorize for you. The power of choice is in you. Nothing or anyone can or will harm you less you accept their negativity, even though the strength of rejection and the persuasion of low self-esteem is very intensified in attacking people's emotions. Neither of them can affect your life in any form if you don't agree to accept the influences of them, so be of good courage.

## REJECTION AND LOW SELF-ESTEEM TEST?

Do you appreciate the appearance of your body? In other words, do you like the look that God gave you? Are you ashamed of your self-image? Do you wish that you were some- one else? What value do you apply to yourself? If you don't know your value, then you will consent and accept some- one's mark-down evaluation and worth of you.

Do you see yourself as an attractive person? Do you believe that you are fantastic in spite of your many mistakes? Any person who invests in unhealthy feelings concerning their self-image will not be happy with their reflection. When a person is experiencing low self-esteem and self-rejection, you will never be satisfied with yourself or your likeness.

A person who doesn't love and accept his or her self-image will reject their original appearance to seek another, taking on the image that meets other people's approval.

The voice of rejection and low self-esteem is completely deceptive in reasoning. It always speaks to us only of the things to which we can relate and which makes a lot of sense to us. It motivates our thoughts and imaginations with what is logical, but with the intent to lure us into the bondage of insecurity and resentful feelings. Break the chains of rejection and low self-esteem off your emotion. Mute rejection's voice, and press the play button of God's appreciation of YOU.

## LETTING GO OF THE FEARS OF REJECTION & MOVING INTO TRUE LOVE

Terminate the imaginations of anxiety and the thoughts of low self-esteem, which has painted a picture of emptiness and deceived you into thinking that where you are, is where you are destined to be. It does not mean because you have engaged and invested in both of them for many years that you cannot start over.

You definitely can! Starting over is never easy, especially when you have already put your whole heart into something or someone. Many times people die without fulfilling their God-given purpose because they were fearful of moving forward, out of limited productivity. They chose to disregard reality and continue to invest in falsehood, which was and still is a result of self-rejection. These negative feelings have caused people to be oblivious to their God-given gifts and abilities.

# HOW TO LIVE IN VICTORY AFTER A LIFE OF REJECTION

G enerally, when a person gets disqualified, it's because the disqualifier viewed that person through their own personal bias standards lens, minimizing that person's value. Do not accept anyone's devalued appraisal of you. Always try to remember that you are a worthy vessel which is qualified for God's love.

Do not allow your emotions to become immersed in the hurts of rejection. What your mindset accommodates, your feelings will accumulate and showcase. If you are afflicted and affected by rejection or low self-esteem, you must dig deep and find the courage to overcome. Stop believing rejection and low self-esteem's evaluation of you.

Good courage is required to activate divine faith, with such you will become able to embrace the realm of survival. Don't invest in hopelessness or the feeling of bondage that can intimidate and convince you to believe the inaccurate evaluation of yourself.

Low self-esteem is more than how you feel about yourself. It also relates to the advancement of the skills that you possess. *In* **Joshua 1:7** *(KJV), it* says ***"Only be thou strong and very courageous, that thou mayest observe to do according to all the law, which Moses my servant commanded thee: turn not from it to the right hand or to the left, that thou mayest prosper whithersoever thou goest."***

As stated earlier in this book, low self-esteem's purpose is to negatively influence your mindset, through unprogressive thoughts and emotions. Low self-esteem causes people to live in fear and die without maximizing their gifts and abilities. The need is urgent for people to stop listening to the voices of rejection and low self-esteem. It is therefore vital that these thoughts and the persuasion of fear be eradicated from one's mindset in order to prolong a lifestyle of enjoyment.

## BELIEVE THAT YOU'RE AN EXTREMELY WORTHY PERSON

If you surrender your emotions to the negative valuation of others, then you will never be happy and will always live your life according to other people's standards. The only person that genuinely has the power to stop you from becoming a person of value is you.

The devil will go to great lengths to destroy you. He will use people to attack and discourage you because he sees and knows your value and the great destiny that God has planned for you.

Your rejection of others is not because you are unworthy, but because you are precious and unique. There is not another person like you. You are special. The influence of low self-esteem seeks to hold you in its captivity of no self-worth because the devil recognizes that you have a great destiny. Don't allow the devil or anyone to stop you through rejection turmoil and low self-esteem unproductive feelings.

He wants to deceive you into believing that you are a "nobody." But declare that you're an extremely worthy person, you are not a useless person. There is a diamond mine locked up in you, waiting for you to explore. I hope that you will not doubt your value and worth in God's sight. The resounding theme here is that: YOU ARE WONDERFULLY MADE!

The book of **Luke, Chapter 12:6-7 (KJV)** states, *"Are not five sparrows sold for two farthings, and not one of them is forgotten before God? But even the hairs of your head are all numbered. Fear not, therefore: ye are of more value than many sparrows."* I repeat there is a diamond mine locked within you, waiting for you to explore.

# THE ULTIMATE CURE FOR REJECTION

The ultimate remedy for denial, low self-esteem, depression, oppression, bitterness, lack of forgiveness, hate, fear, deception, selfishness, pride and anger, is love. No prayer meeting, Bible studies, preaching, teaching, dancing or singing can deliver you from rejection. Only the love of God can do that. *Love "suffereth" long*, meaning that love opposed the idea to give up on hope. It is not hasty to quit in troublesome times; love maintains patience in every affliction of life.

Jesus uses love to defeat Satan, who is the spirit of rejection, and all of his demonic forces. It is the will of God for you to enjoy yourself in his love because He created you in his image after his likeness. He knows that if you don't enhance your life with love, that rejection would invade your mindset and enslave your emotion into all of its ruin energy. Through his love for us, God has also commanded that we love others in the same manner as we love ourselves. Love is our defence and protection against the disqualification of one another.

Love will prevent the division of rejection and promote unity. Hate is the fuel of rejection that causes our emotions to become a furnace of anger, and only love alone can put out that flame of hurt. That is why Jesus says to love them that hate you, because love will shield you from all the scornful feeling of hate and resentment.

# PERFECT LOVE IS THE ANTIDOTE FOR FEAR OF REJECTION

How many times have you told yourself that you are over the hurt of rejection, but when a challenge arises, or you get tested, you realize that you are still living in subjection of the fear of rejection? In spite of every setback and failure you may have experienced from your past to present time, you "**must**" combat the fear of rejection with perfect love and tranquillity of mind. Every day, twenty-four hours a day, to maintain continuous freedom from its inner conflicts and pain.

Embrace the power of understanding and appreciation. Once you can see and believe that you are an extraordinary masterpiece, unique in every way. Then, and only then will you start to become grateful and extremely thankful, that you are worthy of living a loving, peaceful and happy life! Perfect is God, accept God in Christ Jesus, and through HIM!! You will receive power to break every shackle of rejection fear and set your feelings free from the captivity of its hurt.

# CHRIST JESUS IS THE ONLY WAY TO OVERCOME REJECTION

I believe that everyone who is affected or afflicted by rejection and is willing to acquire the mindset of the Lord Jesus Christ, by faith, will be able to break free from rejection and all other negative energy that has been imprisoning them. Christ is the perfect example to overcome rejection.

No one in this world had experienced or will ever go through the level of rejection and pain that Jesus Christ suffered when he became human, to save us from sin and destruction. By his Spirit, He declared through King David in *Psalm 41:7*(NLT), *"All who hate me whisper together against me: against me do they devise my hurt."* You may probably be able to relate to this statement, where your haters did not stop believing the worst of you.

*Psalms 118:22* says, *"The stone which the builders refused becomes the stone of the corner." (NLT).* Jesus, as the son of God, did not permit the rejection of others to cancel or disqualify his mandate. He is completely Unchangeable, Unshakeable and Unstoppable against every assignment of failure that was appointed to prevent him from becoming our Chief Cornerstone. Also, in the book of *Isaiah 53:3* (CLV) it says that, *"He is despised and rejected of men; a man of sorrows and acquainted with grief: and we hid as it were our faces from him; he was despised, and we esteemed him not."*

This Scripture clearly states that Jesus was hated, rejected, and his life was filled with sorrow and terrible suffering. Similar to the experiences that Jesus had, you might be despised, rejected, burdened with grief and suffering with pain.

You may even be scorned continuously by others and disqualified as a "nobody." If that is your experience, don't embrace rejection and the negative energy that comprise it. Embody the mindset and conduct of Jesus Christ. Refuse to allow any form of rejection or scorn to enter into your mindset to corrupt your emotions. Once you have purged all negativity from your mindset, just ask Jesus to be a permanent resident within your feelings.

# CONCLUSION

It is customary and mandatory that whenever there is a conflict with oneself or others, rejection immediately presents its symptoms first. So, when there is an emotional conflict, you have to choose which mindset to pick feelings from as weapons to fight. Unproductive mindsets to select from are rejection, fear, low self-esteem and hatred. The productive mindsets are love, power and soundness, good courage, peace, happiness and love for yourself and others.

Lucifer is very strategic. He is always watching us, and waiting for us to experience a stressful time so that he can influence us to deny hope, and trust in low self-esteem and rejection hurts. *1 Peter 5:5* says that the devil "**goeth about like a roaring lion seeking whomever he may devour**." Don't allow him, yourself, anyone or anything to devour your purpose to live.

Millions of people are depressed, daily falling deeper into hopelessness. They desire a solution to remedy their over-exhausted mindset. I believe that *Philippians 3:13-14* can and will help many to unload their emotions from all the unnecessary waste weight that is compressing the mind. Here is what it says: **"Brethren, I count not myself to have apprehended: this one thing I do forgetting those things which are behind, I press toward the mark for the prize of the high calling of God in Christ Jesus.**

"What is the one thing? It is to forget those things which are behind. The backwards things signify all the negative and positive elements from our past. There are many things from your past that might be positive, but you cannot transfer them into your present, such would slow down your emotional hard drive. Some people desire new things but have no interest in letting the old stuff go. This causes them to keep their mindset in a state of jam-packed feelings. If that's you, get at it and start an emergency clean-up. Dump your past storages out of your emotions and refresh your mindset with the proper understanding of moving forward.

Can we presently forget our past's lifestyle? The answer is no. When you forget something, you have no memory of it. The Apostle Paul was not saying that he has memory loss of the things of his past lifestyle. Forgetting here means to neglect. So, the indication is that he ignored the memories of all the behind things, and did not allow them, to become a hindrance to his newness of life in Christ. Focus on the forward things that Christ purposed for you, and neglect all the behind stuff. For in Christ, we are not subjected to the old self things or negative mindset way of thinking.

You are not to live according to your past analysis of you. Know and believe that in Christ Jesus, you are entirely restored. *2 Corinthians 5:17* says, *"Therefore if any man is in*

***Christ, he is a new creature: old things are passed away; behold, all things become new.***" The behind things are attached to rejection and low self-esteem mobile. But your new stuff is connected to acceptance and high-esteem living. God can part the red sea of rejection and low self-esteem. He can cause you to cross over from years of bondage, hurtful feelings of guilt, pain and shame, into his peace of mind, joy and love. He can bridge all gaps and repair every breach. So, seek to cultivate healthy feelings concerning yourself. Engage in positive self-talk using the holy scriptures. Don't allow feelings of rejection or the negative energy of others, and low self-esteem undervalued feelings to cause you to decline God's testimony of you. The sentiments of Satan are to provide you with, confusion, wickedness thinking, and a sad ending through his rejection relationship. So choose love, and embrace it entirely in your mindset for such is God.

# COMPARISON

Many people look to psychology and behavioural conditioning to help with low self-esteem, which is fantastic. However, this book provides a different viewpoint.

For example: in psychological and behavioural conditioning, a stimulus is presented to cause the person who is affected by low self-esteem to gain some sense of appreciation of themselves.

In such a case, they have to continue receiving that reinforcement.

Let me illustrate if it is an apple that makes the person laugh then to sustain that happiness an apple must be presented at all times. But in the absence of the apple, the person reverts to being sad and broken.

The stimulus that my book offers is of a spiritual nature which causes a person to identify and appreciate the Creator appraisal of them. In light of such acknowledgement, one does not live in the validation of others. But according to their original design in God.

The stimulus that my books seek to promote is also to encourage one to become connected with their own identity through God's valuation of them. Such is revealed in the Holy Scripture.

My book also aims to empower those who are influenced by low self-esteem to become self-liberated. For example, Mary does not know how to cook. So she depends entirely on Suzan to always cook for her, however when Susan is not able to produce food for Mary, then she will experience lack. However, if Mary comes to acknowledge that she has the ability and potential to cook her food and put them in action. Then she would not need to rely on Suzan to prepare a meal for her.

The conclusion is that my book motivates those who live and depend on others to make them feel or look worthy, to acknowledge that they are born noble with the capacity to love and appreciate themselves.

## SOLUTIONS THAT WORK

▶ Daily purging of the mind from every negative effect
▶ Maintain love and appreciation of yourself
▶ Become fully persuaded that though you cannot erase your past, you can overcome it.
▶ Speak over and into your life what you desire to see manifest
▶ Believe wholeheartedly that every disappointment in your life is an opportunity to gain better appointments. And that ever setback is your training ground to advance you into victory.
▶ Refuse to live your life based on other peoples' opinion of what they calculate you to value.
▶ If you don't accept and embrace yourself as a person of worth, then your mindset will not change. From who you understand you to be according to peoples' false views and misleading perception of your true identity.

## GOD RICHLY BLESS YOU.

# REFERENCES

Contemporary English Version Bible (CEV)
American Bible Society (1995)

King James Bible (KJV) Church of England (1611)

New King James Version (NKJV) 1975
Thomas Nelson Publishers

New International Version (NIV) International Bible Society
(1978, 1984)

New Living Translation (NLT) Tyndale House
Publishers(1996)

6) Biblestudy.org
Marie Miguel (How The Happiness Hormone
Works With The Body 2.1.2019)
Better help www.betterhelp.com

AAAS Science NetLinks https//www.aaas.org - oxygen

Write to us @ Kingdom House of Worship
1708 Weston Road North York, Ontario Canada
M9N 1V6

Website: www.kingdomhouseofworship.com

Email: love@kingdomhouseofworship.com

Or Bishopjoel1973@gmail.com
Phone: 647-705-4910